The Essential Guide to SSAT (Upper/Middle) Reading Comprehension

by

J Stevenson

TABLE OF CONTENTS

Why Reading is like Exercising a Muscle 5

The Definition of Reading 6

    Five Types of Reading 8

    Are You a Left-Brain or a Right-Brain Reader? 10

The Eye and its Movements 12

    Eye Span 14

    Peripheral vision 15

The Roots of Slow Reading 16

    Eight Factors that Reduce Reading Rate 16

    How Winners Overcome these Limiting Factors 17

How do Winners Read? 22

    Reading in 'Thought Groups': Fast readers do not read every word. 22

    Ignore words that are unimportant 23

    Take in more words at a time 24

    Rate Adjustment 25

Does Faster Reading Result in Lower Comprehension? 27

    The relationship between the rate of reading and comprehension 27

Winning Techniques and Exercises to Triple Your Reading Speed 30

    Visual Reading Techniques 30

    Visual Configuration 33

Some common Reading Techniques 36

    Skimming 36

    Pacing 37

    Scanning 40

Effective process for In-Depth Reading 42

    Establish Purpose 42

    Survey a Book or Publication 43

    Revise Purpose 44

Study in Depth... 44

Evaluation.. 45

Rapid Reading Techniques 46

The SQ3R Method 46

Key Word Noting.. 48

Taking Notes.. 49

Associative Networks 50

Mind Maps 51

Strips reading 52

Read first sentence 52

Active reading 53

Winning Tips for SSAT Reading Comprehension 55

What is the most effective reading method for SSAT?... 55

How to deal with difficult passages 58

Noticing shifts in Passages 62

Using the 80 - 20 rule to your advantage 63

How to get a hyper focus on the SSAT... 63

Developing Effective Reading Skills for the SSAT.. 65

Aspects of reading - in the context of the SSAT.. 66

Concentration and active reading... 66

Functional reading 66

Looking for information 66

When should you take notes? 67

Types of Passages on the SSAT 69

Question Types & Strategies for tackling them 72

Main Idea/Primary Purpose Questions... 72

Title Questions 74

Specific Detail or Target questions 75

Inference Type Questions 75

Attitude Questions 76

Structure Questions 76

SSAT Reading Comprehension Practice 78

Passage SET 1 78

Passage Set 1: Answers with Explanations 91

PASSAGE SET 2 96

Passage Set 2: Answers with Explanations 129

Why Reading is like Exercising a Muscle

We all have a capacity for reading much faster than we typically do. Our reading speed changes as we go through life.

When we are in school, we go through about two hundred words a minute.

We get to college and, because we have to read faster due to time constraints and a much greater amount to read, we read faster. Most people in college average about 400 words per minute.

Then we get out of college and we don't have to read so fast. There are no longer time constraints, and we can read slow and easy. We find ourselves dropping back down to about 200 words per minute.

Think of reading like you think of a muscle: **the more you read, the better you get at it**, and the faster you're going to read. And we have a great capacity for reading faster. We aren't even scraping the surface of how fast we can read.

You see, we have 1,000,000,000,000 brain cells. In fact, the inner connections, the synapses, in our mind are virtually infinite. It has been estimated by scientists that the number of synapses we have is one followed by 10 million zeros. Our physical capacity for reading is beyond our comprehension. Our visual unit has the capability to take in a full page of text in 1/20 of a second.

If we could turn the pages fast enough, our brain could process it faster than our eyes can see it. If we could turn those pages fast enough, our eyes have the capacity to read a standard book in six to twenty-five seconds depending on the length of the book. We could take in the entire Encyclopedia Britannica in one hour.

So reading 700 - 1,000 words a minute is easily within our reach.

The Definition of Reading

Reading may be defined as an individual's total inter-relationship with symbolic information. Reading is a communication process requiring a series of skills. As such a reading is a **thinking process** rather than an exercise in eye movements. Effective reading requires a logical sequence of thinking or thought patterns, and these thought patterns require practice to set them into the mind. They may be broken down into the following seven basic processes:

> Practice reading to increase your speed. The more you read, the faster you will get.

1. **Recognition**: the reader's knowledge of the alphabetic symbols.
2. **Assimilation**: the physical process of perception and scanning.
3. **Intra-integration:** basic understanding derived from the reading material itself, with minimum dependence on past experience, other than a knowledge of grammar and vocabulary.
4. **Extra-integration:** analysis, criticism, appreciation, selection and rejection. These are all activities that require the reader to bring their past experience to bear on the task.
5. **Retention**: this is the capacity to store the information in memory.
6. **Recall**: the ability to recover the information from memory storage.
7. **Communication**: this represents the application of the information and may be further broken down into at least four categories, which are:
   - Written communication;
   - Spoken communication;
   - Communication through drawing and the manipulation of objects;
   - Thinking, which is another word for communication with the self.

Many problems in reading and learning are due to old habits. Many students still read in the way that they were taught in elementary school. Their reading speed has settled to about 250 words per minute (w.p.m.). Many students can think at rates of 500 w.p.m. or more, so their mind is running at twice the speed of their eyes. A consequence is that it is **easy to lapse into boredom**, daydreaming or thinking about what you want to do on the weekend. Frequently, it is through this type of distraction that you find that you have to re-read sentences and paragraphs, and as a result, ideas are difficult to understand and remember.

The basic problem - the mismatch between thinking fast and reading fast - arises for the most part from the **inadequate methods** by which reading is taught. Since World War II, there have been two main approaches: the Look-Say method and the Phonic method. Both methods are only semi-effective.

In the **Phonic method** a child is first taught the alphabet, then the different sounds for each of the letters, then the blending of sounds and finally, the blending of sounds which form words. This method works best with children who are left-brain dominant.

In contrast, the **Look-Say** method works best with children who are right-brain dominant. With this method, a child is taught to read by presenting the child with cards on which there are pictures of objects, the names of which are printed clearly underneath. By using this method a basic vocabulary is built up, much in the manner of learning to read Chinese. When a child has built up enough basic vocabulary, he progresses through a series of graded books similar to those for the child taught by the **Phonic method**, and eventually becomes a silent reader. In neither of the above cases is a child taught how to read quickly and with maximum comprehension and recall.

Neither the **Look-Say method** nor the **Phonic method**, either in isolation or in combination, are adequate for teaching an individual to read in the complete sense of the word. Both these methods are designed to cover the first stage of reading, the stage of recognition, with some attempt at assimilation and intra-integration. Children are given little help on how to comprehend and integrate the material properly, or on how to ensure it is remembered. The methods currently used in schools do not touch on the problems of speed, retention, recall, selection, rejection, concentration, note taking, and indeed all those skills which can be described as advanced reading techniques.

In short, most of your reading problems have not been dealt with during your initial education. By using appropriate techniques, the limitations of early education can be overcome and reading ability improved by 500% or more.

Five Types of Reading

Scanning type of reading

For example, scanning a directory:

- You are looking for information quickly.
- You know what you are searching for (keywords and names).
- You 'see' every item on the page, but you don't necessarily read the pages - you ignore anything you are not looking for. Thus, when you discover the keywords being searched for, you will be unable to recall the exact content of the page.

Skimming type of reading

You use **skimming** when you read quickly to gain a general impression as to whether the text is of use to you. You are not necessarily searching for a specific item or key words. **Skimming** provides an 'overview' of the text. **Skimming** is useful for looking at chapter or section headings, summaries, and opening paragraphs. The purposes of **skimming** are:

- To check relevance of text.
- To set the scene for the more concentrated effort that is to follow, if the text is useful.

Light type of reading

Reading for leisure tends to be 'light.' **Light reading** involves:

- Reading at a pace that feels comfortable.
- Reading with understanding.
- Skimming the boring, irrelevant passages.

An average light reading speed is 100-200 words per minute. This form of reading does not generally require detailed concentration.

Word by word type reading

This type of reading is time consuming and demands a high level of concentration. Some material is not readily understood and so requires a slow and careful analytical read. People use this type of reading for unfamiliar words and concepts e.g. scientific formulae. It can take up to an hour just to read a few lines of text.

'Reading to study' type of reading

A method of reading for study is called the **SQ3R** method. The aim is to understand the material in some depth. The method involves five simple steps: **Survey, Question, Read, Recall and Review.**

- Survey: skim through to gain an overview, not to understand key points.
- Question: devise questions you hope the text will answer.
- Read: slowly and carefully.
- Recall: from memory, write down the main points made by the chapter.
- Review: revisit your questions - compare these to your recall and establish how well the text has answered them; fill in any gaps by further reading and note-taking.

Are You a Left-Brain or a Right-Brain Reader?

Recently research was carried out in the United States to determine the difference between a left-brain reader and a right-brain reader. A special apparatus was constructed, consisting of a television screen to present the reading material, with a cursor that the subject had to fixate upon. Eye-movements were monitored electronically, so the cursor would move when the subject moved his eyes. The equipment could be set up in two modes. In the first mode, material to the left of the cursor was blanked out on the screen if the subject attempted to move his fixation point to the right of the cursor. In the second mode, material to the right of the cursor was blanked out if the subject attempted to move his fixation point to the left of the cursor.

In the first (left-brain) mode, when words to the left of the cursor blanked out, preventing the subject from regressing or back-skipping, this duplicated the habitual pattern of a left-brain reader, who always reads one or more words ahead of a particular fixation point. In the second (right-brain) mode, when words to the right of the cursor blanked out, preventing the subject from anticipating by reading one or two words ahead of the fixation point, this duplicated the habitual pattern of a right-brain reader, who tends to re-read the words leading up to a particular fixation point.

This study was conducted on a group of 30 subjects. When the equipment was set up in the left-brain mode, the maximum observed average reading speed of the group was 1600 w.p.m., and when the equipment was set-up in the right brain mode, the maximum observed average reading speed of the group was 95 w.p.m.; a difference of 17:1.

You can learn to become a Left-Brain Reader and significantly increase your reading speed.

Note: with material presented in the left-brain mode, the average reading speed of the group was raised from 500 w.p.m. to 1600 w.p.m.; it more than trebled.

You can quickly test if you are a Left-Brain reader or a Right-Brain reader by following the steps below;

1.   Take a novel and read it silently while running your finger along the line of print as you read it.
2.   Note carefully: How far are you reading ahead of your fixation point? The fixation point is determined by your finger position.
3.   Do you find that it is difficult to read ahead of the fixation point? Do you find that you are holding on to the two or three words you have just read?

If the answer to number 2 is yes, and you are reading ahead of the fixation point, you are a left-brain reader. If the answer to number 3 is yes, and attention is drawn back to the words that you have already read, then you are a right-brain reader.

The Eye and its Movements

In order to understand how we read and how reading may be improved, we must first look at how the eye works. Light entering the eye is focused by the lens onto the retina, which lines the inside of the eye. The retina itself consists of hundreds of millions of tiny cells responsive to light. Some cells - the cones - respond to specific colors; others - the rods - to the overall light intensity. These cells are connected to a web of nerves extending over the retina, which relay information to the visual cortex. The center of the retina, called the fovea, is a small area in which the cells are much more tightly packed, so that the perception of images falling on the fovea is much sharper and more detailed than elsewhere on the retina. When we focus our attention on something, the light from that item is focused onto the fovea - this is called a fixation.

A reader's eyes do not move over print in a smooth manner. If they did, they would not be able to see anything, because the eye can only see things clearly when it can hold them still. If an object is still, the eye must be still in order to see it, and if an object is moving, the eye must move with the object in order to see it. **When you read a line, the eyes move in a series of quick jumps and still intervals**. The jumps themselves are so quick as to take almost no time, but the fixations can take anywhere from a quarter to one and a half seconds. At the slowest speeds of fixation a student's reading speed is less than one hundred w.p.m.

Thus, the eye takes short gulps of information. In between it is not actually seeing anything; it is moving from one point to another. We do not notice these jumps because the information is held over in the brain and integrated from one fixation to the next so that we can perceive a smooth flow. The eye is rarely still for more than half a second. Even when you feel the eye is completely still (as when you look steadily at a fixed point such as the following comma), it will in fact be making a number of small movements around the point. If the eye were not constantly shifting in this way, and making new fixations, the image would rapidly fade and disappear. The untrained eye spends about a quarter of a second at each point of fixation, so it is limited to about four fixations per second. Each fixation of an average reader will take in two or three words, so that to read a line on this page probably takes between three and six fixations. The duration of the stops and the number of words taken in by each fixation will vary considerably depending on both the material being read and the individual's reading skill.

> Developing your peripheral vision can allow your eyes to perceive words ahead of your fixation point, and increase your reading speed.

Although the sharpest perception occurs at the fovea, images that are off-center are still seen, but less clearly. **This peripheral vision performs a very valuable function during reading.** Words that lie ahead of the current point of fixation will be partially received by the eye and transmitted to the brain. This is possible because words can be recognized when they are in peripheral vision and the individual letters are too blurred to be recognized. On the basis of this slightly blurred view of what is coming, the brain will tell the eye where to move to next. Thus, the eye does not move along in a regular series of jumps, but skips redundant words and concentrates on the most significant (useful and distinguishing) words of the text. **Immediate memory span depends on the number of 'chunks' rather than the information content.** When we read, we can take in about five chunks at a time. A chunk may be a single letter, a syllable, a word, or even a small phrase - the easier it is to understand, the larger will be the chunks.

In the case of a skilled reader, the fixation points tend to be concentrated toward the middle of a line of print. When the eye goes to a new line, it does not usually start at the beginning, instead it starts a word or two from the edge. The brain has a good idea of what is to come from the sense of the previous lines and only needs to check with peripheral vision to verify that the first few words are as anticipated. Similarly, the eye usually makes its last fixation a word or two short of the end of a line, again making use of peripheral vision to check that the last few words are as expected. The rhythm and flow of the faster reader will carry him comfortably through the meaning, whereas the slow reader will be far more likely to become bored and lose the meaning of what he is reading. A slow reader, who pauses at every word and skips back reading the same word two or three times, will not be able to understand much of what he reads. By the end of a paragraph the concept is lost, because it is so long since the paragraph was begun. During the process of rereading, his ability to remember fades, and he starts doubting his ability to remember at all. There is a dwindling spiral of ability. The person re-reads more, then loses more trust in his memory and finally concludes that he doesn't understand what he is reading.

For over a hundred years, experts in the field of medical and psychological research have concluded that most humans only use from 4% to 10% of their mental abilities - of their potential to learn, to think and to act. Speeding up a process such as reading is an effective method of enabling a student to access a larger proportion of the 90-95% of the mental capacity that he is not using. When a person is reading rapidly, he is concentrating more, and when he can raise his speed of reading above about 500 w.p.m., with maximum comprehension, he is also speeding up his thinking. New depths of the brain become readily accessible. In addition, accelerated reading can reduce fatigue. Faster reading also improves comprehension, because the reader's level of concentration is higher, and there is less cause for him to develop physical tensions such as a pain in the neck or a headache. A further benefit is the improvement of the completeness of thought.

For example, try watching a 90 minute video in nine ten-minute sections; comprehension will be much less than it would be had the video been presented in its entirety. There is an optimum reading speed for maximum comprehension, which is proportional to your top speed. This rate will vary from one type of material to another, and finding the best rate for the material you are reading is critical for good comprehension.

Eye Span

OK, what do we do? Well, there are several things we are going to do to increase reading speed. First of all, we are going to increase the **EYE SPAN.** Eye span is the **number of words** that you take in as you look at the words. In other words, if my eye span is just one word, I am going to move from word to word to word. If my eye span is two words, I am going to move along twice as fast. If my eye span is three words, three times as fast. If I am moving along in phrases, I'm flying along pretty good. That's where you increase the rate of eye span.

> The number of words you take in when you look at a page is your EYE SPAN.

You also want to learn to work in **THOUGHT UNITS**. Thought units help you move faster. This is where you group the words according to context. For instance, let's say you have "He said something." It's easy to put that in a phrase, then you move to the next phrase. Now consider this sentence: "It's safe to say that almost anyone can double his speed of reading while maintaining equal or higher comprehension." If you wanted to read that sentence in phrases, you might parse it out something like this: "It's safe to say that almost anyone.......can double his speed........of reading while maintaining.......equal or even higher comprehension." You move much faster that way.

So, we are going to increase the number of words we see and we are going to group them according to context. One of the key issues that we are also going to work on is **RETURN EYE SWEEP**. When you get to the end of the sentence or the end of the line on the written page, if your eye meanders back to the other side you have a chance to pick up words. If you're picking up words and you're sight reading, things can get confusing. So you want to dramatically, quickly, and forcefully, go from the end of one line to the beginning of the next. Using a fingertip or pen as a pointer is a great way to move quickly and directly to the next line.

Peripheral vision

When your eyes move down a central strip of the text, you also engage much more of your peripheral vision. That, in turn, brings the right hemisphere of the brain into the reading process. You make much more use of the right brain's ability to synthesize and build relationships within the material. Fast reading is not just about enabling you to read faster; it also allows you to access much more of the brain and thereby increases your comprehension and creativity.

You can also benefit from participation in sports. Sports strengthen crucial reading abilities such as tracking, peripheral vision, focusing, eye teaming, and eye-hand coordination. Participation in sports also improves near- and far-point vision. Many of these skills are not typically learned during sustained computer use though they are essential for both computer use and reading.

The Roots of Slow Reading

You already possess the ability to rapidly read essential information. It is an innate ability. Let me prove this to you. Think about how much information your brain must process while driving an automobile on a highway. It must view and analyze the motions of the surrounding cars, road conditions, weather conditions, read signs, and at the same time avoid hitting animals or people who might cross the road. Instead of being overwhelmed by all this information you become so bored that you might turn on the radio, talk to other passengers, or make cell phone calls. If your brilliant brain is so adept at swiftly reading a road during a drive, then why can't it read text just as quickly and easily? The answer is simple. Instead of seeing a book during reading, your brain hears a voice that pronounces the word sounds printed on the page. Quite simply, you don't see a book, you hear it. Yet, vision is faster and more powerful than hearing. By becoming a more visual reader you will instantly increase your reading speed.

Eight Factors that Reduce Reading Rate

Some of the main factors that reduce reading rate are:

(a) **limited perceptual span** i.e., word-by-word reading;

(b) **slow perceptual reaction time**, i.e., slowness of recognition and response to the material;

(c) **vocalization**, including the need to vocalize in order to achieve comprehension;

(d) **faulty eye movements**, including inaccuracy in placement of the page, in return sweep, in rhythm and regularity of movement, etc.;

(e) **regression**, both habitual and as associated with habits of concentration;

(f) **faulty habits** of attention and concentration, beginning with simple inattention during the reading act and faulty processes of retention; poor evaluation of which aspects of the material are important and which are unimportant; and

(g) **lack of practice** in reading, due simply to the fact that the person has read very little and has limited reading interests so that very little reading is practiced in the daily or weekly schedule;

(h) **fear of losing comprehension**, causing the person to suppress his rate deliberately in the firm belief that comprehension is improved if he spends more time on the individual words; the effort to remember everything rather than to remember selectively.

> Lack of practice is a key reason for slow reading rates. Practice your reading to increase your speed.

Since these conditions also reduce comprehension, increasing the reading rate through eliminating them is likely to result in increased comprehension as well. This is an entirely different matter from simply speeding up the rate of reading without reference to the conditions responsible for the slow rate. In fact, simply speeding the rate, especially through forced acceleration, may actually result in making the real reading problem more severe. In addition, forced acceleration may even destroy confidence in ability to read. The obvious solution, then is to increase rate as a part of a total improvement of the whole reading process.

How Winners Overcome these Limiting Factors

Overcoming Subvocalization

Stop talking to yourself when you read. When you read, are you aware of an inner voice that follows the words as your eyes move across the page or the computer screen? This inner voice is called **'subvocalization'.** You probably experience it as a slight movement in the tongue or throat region. As long as you **subvocalize**, you limit your reading to the speed of normal speech, to about 300 w.p.m.

> If you use an inner voice as you read, with movement of the throat or tongue, you are sub-vocalizing. This slows you down.

Some readers need to hear every word with their inner voice; this limits reading speed. This is called the sound barrier. Functional images of the brain show that a concrete word like 'book' preferentially activates visual areas while an abstract word like 'efficiency' is mainly processed by auditory areas, so words do not always require sound to produce meaning. Not faced with this sound barrier, and without special training, deaf people often read above 1000 wpm.

Don't Read Aloud to Yourself. Generally, reading aloud to yourself does not help you study more effectively. If you move your lips while you read, you're not reading efficiently. If you read aloud or move your lips while you're reading, you are reading slowly, so stop moving your lips. Try putting a finger over your lips. Your finger will remind you not to move your lips. Make an effort to read faster and retain more - after a while, you'll be surprised how little effort it will take.

Getting back to reading and how we learn, one of the biggest reasons why we learned to read incredibly slowly in the first place is that as a child in school, we learned to read by sounding out the words. When you pronounce the words you have to read with your tongue. The tongue can only pronounce about 200 to 400 words a minute. According to the 'latest' research, our memory is not stored in our tongue!

While reading, people talk to themselves in two ways:

- **Vocalizing**, which is the actual moving of your lips as you read,
- **Subvocalizing**, which is talking to yourself in your head as you silently read.

Both of these will slow you down to the point that you can't read any faster than you can speak. Speech is a relatively slow activity; for most, the average speed is about 250 w.p.m.

Reading should be an activity that involves only the eyes and the brain. Vocalization ties reading to actual speaking. Try to think of reading as if you were looking at a landscape, a panorama of ideas, rather than looking at the rocks at your feet.

Something that was very helpful for me (in going from above average to really fast) was to catch myself when I find that I'm subvocalizing what I'm reading, i.e. "hearing" all the words spoken. This needless practice automatically slows me down to the speed of spoken English.

To prevent myself from subvocalizing, I try to get a tune stuck in my head, which occupies the auditory centers and lets "me" get on with my reading in peace.

Paul Druery (SSAT Verbal: 99th percentile)

Moving one's lips is rare today, but it is a form of subvocalizing. The first proof occurred at UCLA in the 1960s. Scientists took students and, with permission, placed EMG (Electromyography) connections on the outside of their vocal cords. These connections registered every word as the students read silently. Today scientists use 'fMRIs' (functional Magnetic Resonance Imagery) scans, and see all the 'speech' brain structures light-up with blood-flow, a sign of activity, when students and adults read "silently".

On March 17, 2004, NASA reported that for the first-time in scientific research, they had monitored at-a-distance, human "subvocalization". The title of the report was: NASA Develops System To Computerize Silent, 'Subvocal Speech'. Not only does subvocalization exist, soon spies will be reading what you are thinking.

Someone said that repeating a single word in his mind every time he read, over a six-month period, did the trick for him. I couldn't help but wonder if there was a quicker way to achieve this, so the next time I read and found myself subvocalizing, here is what I did to stop: I increased the rate at which my eyes moved across the page to the point where it was impossible to subvocalize. I switched into a reading mode whereby I noticed gulps of words at each eye resting point. These gulps involved pulling words from multiple lines. I noticed that I was still understanding what I was reading but in a different way.

I caught myself thinking: "But now I'm not really reading." In other words, part of my mind still believed that the definition of reading was to look at every word and sound it out in my mind. A better way to look at this issue is that you should develop multiple reading strategies, some of which may include subvocalization and some may not. See->Understand seems much more efficient than See->Say->Understand.

A handy way to increase your reading rate is to adjust the focus of your eyes (or attention). Look at any nearby image and zoom in on a particular aspect, like the button on a shirt. Then adjust the focus of your eyes so you can see the entire shirt. That's the process you can use to increase your reading speed by increasing the number of words you take in at each eye stop.

Mark Leighton (SSAT Verbal: 99th percentile)

Chunk Four Words

Humans cannot mentally-speak four words at the same time, just one at a time. When we chunk - for example, treat "Power belongs to learners" as if it were a single-word: "Powerbelongstolearners" - we short-circuit subvocalizing that requires us to pronounce a single word, and then the next, and the next, linearly.

Chunking is the process of choosing to take in groups-of-words by panning across our peripheral vision left, center, and right. The more we scratch the old record by taking in words simultaneously – three to four at a time - the more we distort the sounding-out of words and subvocalization dies a slow-death.

Overcoming REGRESSIONS

Regression is going back over words. You can call it back-skipping if you want. You go back over words you previously read. People do it for two reasons. Initially we "regress" in order to clarify the meaning of what we're reading. We want to be sure of the words we read as we go along. In our early years in school, when we were first taught - incorrectly - to "read slowly and carefully," it became easy to go back over words.

Some people regress or back-skip to clarify what they are reading. This hurts their reading speed.

This not only slows you down, it causes you comprehension problems. For instance, let's say you have this sentence: "The man jumped over the log." If you back-skip, you read that passage like this: "The man jumped," "The man . . . jumped. . . over the log," "jumped over the log." So, what your brain is processing is "The man jumped," "The man jumped," "jumped over the log." Our brain is used to processing our flaws, so the brain thinks, "OK, I know what this clown is saying, 'The man jumped over the log.'" But this takes time to sort out. And it's confusing. Think how much easier it would be if you simply took the sentence in, in one sight: "The man jumped over the log." There's no confusion there. Then you move on to the next phrase. Regressing or back-skipping is the most harmful thing we do to slow our reading speed.

Overcoming faulty habits

Our second obstacle is that we have **BAD HABITS** that we have picked up over the years. Bad habits manifest themselves in a number of ways. For one, you've got people who have **MOTOR** habits as they read. These are the people who are tapping a pencil when they read, tapping a foot when they read, moving a book, flicking their hands, and the like. If they're sitting next to you, they drive you nuts. But they are the people who have to be moving while they read. Some may even move their lips. If they do that, they're kind of edging over into another bad habit where we find **AUDITORY** readers. This is a bad habit that is the hardest to drop. Auditory reading is difficult to beat because we are used to reading and hearing the words in our minds. Some people even go so far as to mumble the words. You can see their lips moving sometimes, or you can even hear the guttural growl as they go through the words.

The other obstacles are the **FIXATIONS**. Fixations are the actual stops or pauses between eye-spans when the eye is moving to its next fixation point. We can't see while the eye moves so we need the fixation points to see. The problem is, most people fixate word by word by word. They stop their eyes on each separate word. The fixations slow them down because they are stopping on each word. The problem that comes up here is that, like the other obstacles, it impedes concentration and comprehension as well. The paradox with reading slowly is that it really hurts your concentration.

How do Winners Read?

Reading in 'Thought Groups': Fast readers do not read every word.

Fast readers do not read every word. But, I hear you say, "What if I miss something?" You do not have to read every individual word to follow a text. As an example, try the text below:

F_st r__d_rs s_l_ct w_rds, and they r__d gr_ups of w_rds. R_th_r th_n r__d_ng fr_m l_ft to r_ght, f_st r__d_rs w_l m_ve th__r _y_s _p _nd d_wn th_ p_g_ t_ f_nd th_ _mp_rt_nt w_rds. Th__r m_tive is n_t to und_rst_nd ev_ry w_rd, r_ther it is to s_ek _nswers.

The paragraph above says: "Fast readers select words, and they read groups of words. Rather than reading from left to right, fast readers will move their eyes up and down the page to find the important words. Their motive is not to understand every word, rather it is to seek answers. "

In order to avoid reading every word you can practice increasing the rate your eyes move across the page. Rather than reading from left to right, fast readers will move their eyes up and down the page to find the important words. Fast readers select words, and they read groups of words. Their motive is not to understand every word, rather it is to seek answers. Effective readers will adjust their reading speed. Sometimes they will skim; sometimes they will read carefully. They also predict what they are likely to learn next.

The single major secret of fast reading is to be aware of as you read, to focus above the words, and keep sweeping your eyes from extreme-left, to the center, and to extreme-right. Once more – until it becomes a habit – automatic, with its own neuropath way in your brain. You **will** your eyes to focus above the sentences and sweep across each sentence, left-center-right.

Don't you will yourself to stand-up and walk over to the refrigerator for a soda? Will is another word for choosing to do something you want. It requires practice to turn it on auto-pilot, but focusing above the words and sweeping left-center-right is the top secret of fast reading.

Ignore words that are unimportant

When reading, you may often come upon a word or phrase that you don't understand. Your first impulse may be to look up the word in your dictionary. Before resorting to a dictionary, though, you should first determine whether the word you don't know is important. If it isn't, then ignore it.

Phrase reading

As you lessen the number of times your eyes fix on a line, you will learn to omit unnecessary words. As your eyes are trained to read quickly across a page, your comprehension rates should improve. You will more readily recognize ideas and concepts as well as relationships. When you were taught to read as a child, you probably learned to blend letters together to make a word. **Phrase reading** takes that process a little further by combining words into phrases.

When you first practice phrase reading, read the words in a cluster, as suggested in the following passage. As you practice both the mental and the physical levels of scanning, you will find that your concentration improves. If you don't subvocalize, don't read word-by-word, and don't regress, you will read very efficiently.

Phrase reading allows you to take in groups of words rather than one word at a time.

Many people read very quickly but do not understand what they read. If you practice eye movement exercises, you are practicing the physical level of reading. When you practice phrase-reading, you are attending to the mental level of reading. Ideas are recognized more easily when you read words in a cluster rather than reading one word at a time.

When you learn to phrase-read quickly, you will find that you are able to **skip over many predictable words** in your reading. As your concentration improves, so will your comprehension and understanding.

Take in more words at a time

Fast Reading does not replace regular reading. Most people read one word at a time, saying the word to themselves. This is a slow way of doing the task, especially when your mind is capable of processing information at a much higher rate.

Develop a wider **eye-span** and you read more than one word at a glance. Since written material is less meaningful if read word by word, this will help you learn to read by phrases or thought units. If you normally see two words at a time when you read, your eyes look at two words, move to the next two and stop to look at those, move to the next two, and so on. Begin taking in three words at a time so your eyes make fewer stops, increasing your speed. Challenge yourself by taking in even more words as your skill increases. Keep it fun. Don't push yourself so hard that it becomes stressful.

Many of the words used in writing grammatically correct sentences actually convey no meaning. If, in reading, you exert as much effort in conceptualizing these meaningless words as you do important ones, you limit not only your reading speed but your comprehension as well. A great way to distill meaning out of a paragraph is to take brief notes.

Try to avoid focusing on every word, but rather look at groups of two to three words.

For instance, this sentence could be grouped in this manner:

for instance / this sentence / could be grouped / in this manner

Work on vocabulary improvement. Familiarize yourself with new words so you don't get stuck on them when you read them again.

Rate Adjustment

Poor results are inevitable if the reader attempts to use the same rate indiscriminately for all types of material and for all reading purposes. He must learn to adjust his rate to his purpose in reading and to the difficulty of the material he is reading. This ranges from a maximum rate on easy, familiar, interesting material or when reading to gather information on a particular point, to a minimal rate on material which is unfamiliar in content and language structure, or which must be thoroughly digested. The effective reader adjusts his rate; the ineffective reader uses the same rate for all types of material.

Adjust your reading rate based on what you are reading and your requirements for the reading material.

Rate adjustment may be an overall adjustment to the article as a whole, or internal adjustment within the article. Overall adjustment establishes the basic rate at which the total article is read; internal adjustment involves the necessary variations in rate for each varied part of the material. As an analogy, suppose you plan to take a 100-mile mountain trip. Since this will be a relatively hard drive with hills, curves, and a mountain pass, you decide to take three hours for the total trip, averaging about 35 miles an hour. This is your overall rate adjustment. However, in actual driving you may slow down to no more than 15 miles per hour on some curves and hills, while speeding up to 50 miles per hour or more on relatively straight and level sections. This is your internal rate adjustment. There is no set rate, therefore, at which the good reader follows inflexibly in reading a particular selection, even though he has set himself an overall rate for the total job.

Overall rate adjustment should be based on your **reading plan**, your **reading purpose**, and the nature and difficulty of the material. The reading plan itself should specify the general rate to be used. This is based on the total "size up" of the material and purpose in reading. It may be helpful to consider examples of how purpose can act to help determine the rate to be used. To understand information, skim or scan at a rapid rate. To determine the value of material or to read for enjoyment, read rapidly or slowly according to your feeling. To read analytically, read at a moderate pace to permit interrelating ideas to form in your mind. The nature and difficulty of the material requires an adjustment in rate in conformity with your ability to handle that type of material. Obviously, the level of difficulty is highly relative to the particular reader. While Einstein's theories may be extremely difficult to most laymen, they may be very simple and clear to a professor of physics. Hence, the layman and the physics professor must make a different rate adjustment in reading the same material. Generally, difficult material will entail a slower rate; simpler material will permit a faster rate.

Internal rate adjustment involves selecting differing rates for parts of a given article. In general, **decrease speed** when you find the following: (1) unfamiliar terminology not clear in context; try to understand it in context at that point; otherwise, read on and return to it later; (2) difficult sentence and paragraph structure; slow down enough to enable you to untangle the material and get accurate context for the passage; (3) unfamiliar or abstract concepts; look for applications or examples of your own as well as studying those of the writer; take enough time to get them clearly in mind; (4) detailed, technical material; this includes complicated directions, statements of difficult principles, and materials on which you have scant background; and (5) material on which you want detailed retention.

In general, increase speed when you meet the following: (a) simple material with few ideas which are new to you; move rapidly over the familiar ones; spend most of your time on the unfamiliar ideas; (b) unnecessary examples and illustrations; since these are included to clarify ideas, move over them rapidly when they are not needed; (c) detailed explanations and idea elaborations that you do not need; and (d) broad, generalized ideas and ideas which are restatements of previous ones. These can be readily grasped, even with scan techniques.

In keeping your reading flexible, adjust your rate sensitivity from article to article. It is equally important to adjust your rate within a given article. Practice these techniques until a flexible reading rate becomes second nature to you.

Does Faster Reading Result in Lower Comprehension?

The relationship between the rate of reading and comprehension

Research shows that there is little relationship between reading rate and **comprehension**. Some people read rapidly and comprehend well; others read slowly and comprehend poorly. There is some reason to believe that the factors producing slow reading are also involved in lowered comprehension.

In observing thousands of individuals taking reading training, it has been found in most cases that an increase in rate has been paralleled by an increase in comprehension, and that where rate has gone down, comprehension has also decreased. Although there is at present little statistical evidence, it seems that plodding word-by-word analysis (or word reading) inhibits understanding.

> Comprehension is based on your ability to extract and retain ideas, not on your speed.

Whether you have good comprehension depends on whether you can extract and retain the important ideas of reading, not on how fast you read. If you can do this, you can also increase your reading speed. If you "clutch up" when trying to read fast, or skim and worry about comprehension, your rate and comprehension will drop because the mind is occupied with your fears and you are not paying attention to the ideas that you are reading.

If you **concentrate** on the purpose of reading (locating main ideas and details, and **forcing yourself** to stick to the task of finding them quickly) your speed and comprehension should increase. Your concern should be not with how fast you can get through a chapter, but with how quickly you can locate the facts and ideas that you need.

Most adults are able to increase their rate of reading considerably and rather quickly without lowering comprehension. These same individuals seldom show an increase in comprehension when they reduce their rate. In other cases, comprehension is actually better at higher rates of speed. Such results are heavily dependent upon the method used to gain the increased rate.

Simply reading more rapidly without actual improvement in basic reading habits usually results in lowered comprehension.

Comprehension during fast reading is in many ways easier than during standard reading. Firstly, the mind is busy looking for meaning, not rereading words and sentences. The average reader spends about 1/6th of the time they spend reading actually rereading words. Rereading interrupts the flow of comprehension and slows down the process.

The second advantage is that, on a logical level, you use the knowledge of the subject to fill in needed information by looking at one or two paragraphs. Meanwhile, on a visual level, you absorb up to a page of information and process it. This stimulates many areas of the brain.

Research has shown a close relation between speed and understanding. In checking progress charts of thousands of individuals taking reading training, its been found that in the vast majority of cases, that an increase in reading rate has also been paralleled by an increase in comprehension. The plodding word by word analysis actually reduces comprehension.

In this day and age, our brains are used to constant stimulation. So when we are reading along slowly and carefully, it's kind of like watching a movie encountering a slow motion scene. The slow motion scene is kind of interesting at first because the movie has been moving along at a rapid clip and now we have a change of pace. We've got the slow motion scene of the guy getting shot or the couple running across to each other across a field, and the mind initially says, "Oh, this is cool. This is something different." After a while we get a little impatient and we're ready for the guy who got shot to hit the ground, or the couple who are running across the field to finally get to each other. We start thinking about other things - we've lost our focus on the movie.

The brain does the same thing when we read. The brain is getting all the stimulation it normally gets, then we hit this patch where we're reading slowly. And boom, the brain says, "I don't like this. I think I'm going to start thinking about something else." And the reader starts thinking about their favorite show or the game they hope to have Saturday night. And therefore, you've got another impediment to comprehending the reading correctly.

Test of Reading Speed

Choose a novel or book that you are interested in and can read easily. Measure the time it takes to read five pages. Your reading fast can then be calculated using the following formula: w.p.m. (speed) = (number of pages read) times (number of words per average page), divided by (the number of minutes spent reading).

Winning Techniques and Exercises to Triple Your Reading Speed

Visual Reading Techniques

Ineffectual reading typically leaves out visually constructed imagery from the thought-stream. As a result, the reader has a poor memory and poor contextual analysis skills. Without imagery to reality-check one's comprehension, one may pass a totally anomalous word and fail to notice that it does not fit. Once the reader has a richly detailed internal picture, which includes color, sound and movement, he will no longer be able to read past words and concepts that obviously do not make sense, because these will seem strange in the picture or movie that he has made. For example, a student reads: "The child was made to do the math problem in front of the class upon the skateboard." From his prior picture of a classroom, the student will realize immediately that the word should be "blackboard," instead of "skateboard," and will self-edit the word.

Incorporating visual reading techniques will increase your retention.

One of the characteristics of visual storage is speed, so increasing the pace at which material is covered, with the assistance of speed-reading exercises, usually increases the power of **visualization.** Those students who can adapt to the visual mode of representation successfully are multi-sensory; however, there are some students who have difficulty. These are students who have failed to make the transition between an auditory mode of representation and a visual mode of representation. In normal development this transition occurs at about the age of ten. In the case of these students, retention can be so poor that one sentence later they are unable to remember what they have read. These students will attempt to retrieve the rote sound of words; they will try to store an auditory sequence of the word without transferring the words into pictures in their minds. A student with this problem will frequently state, "I don't remember what it said."

It is now known that **reading involves both sides of the brain:** the left side specializes in coding and decoding, the right side in synthesis of overall meaning. By using this as an operational definition, you can determine which side of a student's brain is deficient when diagnosing his reading ability, and it can be used to formulate a prescriptive plan of how to improve his reading. For example, when a student is able to code and pronounce words disproportionately to his comprehension, his left brain is working in excess of his right brain.

The following **technique** addresses those students who fall in between the two extremes of the good visualizer and the student who has no visual capacity at all:

1. The first step is to check that you have the ability to picture objects and relationships in your mind's eye. Look at your desk and pretend that this desk is really your bedroom, and that you are on the ceiling, looking down at the four walls and everything contained inside. Mentally point to the wall where the bed is, the walls with windows, the door, the shelves, and so on. Do this exercise again with the layout of the whole house. This exercise will validate that you can make mental pictures of concrete objects, a right-brain skill.

2. Read a phrase or sentence out loud. The sentence is the easiest grammatical unit to use for this particular method. A sentence should be chosen that uses nouns that are concrete and action verbs, rather than abstract nouns and the verb 'to be', as these will prevent the use of right-brain picturing abilities. As soon as you have stopped reading the sentence, close your eyes and picture in your mind what the sentence described. Notice the color, size, shape, foreground, and distance of the picture in your mind. This will give you a better idea of your basic capacity to visualize. Used as a repetitive exercise, this will improve your visualization.

3. Once you can form a reasonably good mental picture from a sentence you have just read, the next goal is to find how many pictures you can hold on to. Read out between three and nine visualizable sentences. If you go beyond your capacity, you will lose the first and second picture. This will tell you your capacity for a sequence of separate pictures. Practice will improve this ability. Students who find it easy to create pictures and take in large amounts of information have the facility to take information spread out over several pictures and sequence this information **into a movie**. When you can do this well, you will have a seemingly infinite memory capacity, taking advantage of the right brain's incredible powers (you will probably have noticed how much easier it is to remember students' faces than their names).

4. Those who have done little visualization in the past, tend to make pictures that are sparse in detail and poor in quality. They may leave out sub modalities, the major components of our senses. A partial list of sub modalities follows, under the headings of three sensory systems (modalities):

Visual Auditory Kinesthetic

Visual auditory kin aesthetics deals with a number of important aspects of reading and taking full advantage of your ability to visualize when reading. It encompasses the consideration of such things as:

- shapes, volume, and pressure
- colors, pitch, and temperature
- black/white pace of speech and emotions
- movement, number of sounds, and speed of movement
- size, location of sound, and location of felt sensations
- perspective, rhythm, and texture

When reading a novel, many students fail to make adequate use of auditory imagery, even when they are good visualizers. If you use your auditory imagery to give all the '"he said ..." and "she said ..." dialogue, then your memory of the story will be vastly improved. When you read a book and use all the forms of imagery, you will experience the story as a three-dimensional movie in stereophonic sound, with imagery of emotion and movement, touch, taste, and even temperature. You will be totally at one with the book and your subsequent recall will be nearly perfect. You will hardly be aware of reading the words, unless there is a gross printing error.

It may be difficult to construct concrete images when reading abstract material such as philosophy. A student who has both high right-brain and left-brain capacity will tend to form abstract patterns, rather like modern art, to hang the words and pictures upon. Modern physics has little that can be visualized as concrete imagery. However, when a psychologist asked Einstein about his thinking processes, Einstein replied, *'I think in a combination of abstract visual patterns and muscular sensations; it is only later, when I wish to speak or write to another person, that I translate these thoughts into words.'*

Visual Configuration

The other thing that helps us increase our speed is **CONFIGURATION.** As you read faster and faster, you've got to learn to rely on your increased recognition of how words are configured, how they look, as you do it. In other words, "material" looks different than "response". "Recognition" looks different than "perceptual". The words have visual configurations. As you learn to read faster and faster you learn to pick up on the configurations and, as you do better and better, your skills at this improve with practice.

> Learning to quickly recognize word configurations can help increase your reading speed.

So, we are going to have no **REGRESSIONS**, no **VOCALIZATIONS**, and increased **EYE SPAN**. That's the way to true sight reading. How do we do this?

First, we avoid the problem areas. We avoid the limited eye-span by expanding the number of words that we take in. We get rid of regressions and we get rid of the return eye sweep problem by using a pointer. You can use a pen, a pencil, even your finger. That gives you a point of focus for your eyes. It helps you focus on the page, and you move faster because you can dictate how fast you are moving across the page. Your eye will follow your finger, pen, or pencil.

Absolutely stay away from the vocalizations. You have got to be a sight reader. You have got to read fast enough so that you don't have time to hear the words. This way you are comprehending simply with your eyes.

You also need to keep in mind that you don't always read at the same speed. If you've got a car that will go 120 miles per hour, you're not going to drive that car 120 miles per hour in a shopping center. You'd get killed and get a heck of a ticket. But you may, on a highway when you are passing a car, get your car up to a high speed. When you are in that shopping center, you are going to be driving about 30 miles per hour.

It's the same thing with reading. This is specifically addressed in our Better Reading section. But you must learn that you speed read in certain areas and in other areas that may be particularly dense, or that may have something that's particularly confusing to you, you will need to slow down and read in shorter phrases and smaller groupings of words so that you can comprehend it clearly. It may be a particularly dense passage where each word has a great deal of meaning. It may be even an unusual or specific word.

Let's look at what we've got to do to practice it. The big step here is to simply read faster. It sounds like such a simple statement, it almost sounds stupid. But it's what you have to do. You have to focus on "I'm going to read faster," first.

What is Comprehension Lag?

Comprehension comes later. Practice reading without a great concern for comprehension. In clinical terms, we call this the comprehension lag. It takes the mind as many as ten to fifteen days to adapt to the new reading rate. You are going to go through periods, practice periods, you can't use on school books, but they are practice periods where you are simply adapting to reading that much faster. Comprehension lags for a while but when it catches up it makes a stunning difference.

> As you initially learn to increase your reading speed, comprehension will lag behind speed. This is normal.

A good place to practice this is a magazine or newspaper. These have narrow columns that almost make a perfect thought unit. You can go straight down the column, taking that finger and putting it in the middle of the column and moving it straight down the page. You will be stunned by how soon you will be able to improve and comprehend what you are reading that way. You find that it's quick. It's easy reading.

There's always the Dual option: force yourself to read a 500+ page book in one day. Force yourself to read faster via skimming or whatever. I started to use this when I had to read Les Miserables in one day. Sure, I didn't know what the hell happened in the book, but I began to speed read everything and now I can knock out 500+ page novels in a day with decent comprehension. However, thick material such as text books are another problem for me.
Jeremiah Smith (Reading Speed: 1000 wpm)

You already know 90% of the information that you will read. Our brain uses schema for decoding text. Each of us has a lifetime of experiences stored in our memory map. Stored experiences that writers expect us to possess and use while reading.

Let's use an example to learn how you use schema to interpret text. Imagine I wrote a story and told you, "The woman wore a red dress." I would expect you to know what I meant by the word woman. As a reader, you don't expect me to explain to you what a woman is. You already know this information. You are using your schema or life database to read this text.

Keep practicing

You'll be conscious of using it and that may very well distract you a little from comprehending what you're reading. But keep practicing and the technique will become automatic, no longer requiring your conscious attention, allowing you to put your full attention on the content of the written material. At that point, you will have gained an increase in reading skill to enjoy for the rest of your life.

Fast reading is voluntary self-improvement. When you taught yourself to ride a bicycle or play a sport - that was voluntary self-improvement. When you succeeded and did it well, it felt good. Self-improvement is self-development; it feels good and it is good.

Sharper focus

The only way you are going to read faster and understand your reading better is to learn to first tap into this incredible brain power you are gifted with and then second, to build a sharper focus. Once you focus better, your comprehension improves, your recall and memory improves and your appreciation and enjoyment of the reading process are more likely to improve. And the reality is you were probably never taught to focus in school, at work or in college. If you think about reading faster, you will make an effort to pick up the pace. Reading fast is something you must work on and concentrate on until it becomes a habit.

Some common Reading Techniques

Skimming

1. Point with your index finger or a pen to the words you are reading. Try and move your finger faster, this will aid you in establishing a smooth and rhythmical reading habit.

2. As you move your finger along the line that you are reading, try and take in more than one word at a time.

3. When you have reached the limits of the previous exercise, then take some light reading material and try to read more than one line at the same time. Magazine articles are good for this purpose because many magazines have narrow columns of about five or six words, and often the material is light reading.

4. Various patterns of visual guiding should be experimented with. These include diagonal, curving, and straight-down-the-page movements. Exercise your eye movements over the page, moving your eyes on horizontal and vertical planes and diagonally from the upper left of the page to the lower right and finally, from the upper right to the lower left. Try to speed-up gradually day by day. The purpose of this exercise is to train your eyes to function more accurately and independently.

5. Practice reading as fast as you can for one minute, without worrying about comprehension. You don't worry about your comprehension because this is an exercise in perceptual speed.

6. For this exercise you are concerned primarily with speed, although at the same time you are reading for as much comprehension as possible. Reading should continue from the last point reached. Do this for one minute and then calculate your reading speed - call this your highest normal speed.

7. Practice reading (with comprehension) for one minute at approximately 100 w.p.m. faster than your highest normal speed.

8. When you can do that, continue increasing your speed in approximately 100 w.p.m. increments. If you calculate how many words there are on an average line, then it is easy to convert w.p.m. into lines per minute. For example, if a line has ten words and you are reading at one line per second, then you are reading at 600 w.p.m.

9. Start from the beginning of a chapter and practice reading three lines at a time, with a visual aid (such as a card) and at a fast reading rate, for 5 minutes.
10. Read on from this point, aiming for comprehension at the highest speed possible. Do this for five minutes, then calculate and record your reading speed in w.p.m.
11. Take an easy book and start of the beginning of a chapter. Skim for one minute using a visual guide at four seconds per page.
12. Return to the beginning of the chapter and practice reading at your minimum speed for five minutes.

Pacing

The previous **Fast Perception** exercises involving reading three lines at a time or a page in four seconds may be called 'skimming' - this is a superficial way of reading, more a perceptual exercise than reading for meaning.

Pacing, the next reading technique to be learned, describes an unconventional way of reading a page, which can reduce the amount of work by more than half without significantly reducing the comprehension. The following **Pacing** technique is a two-step process that involves collecting related facts and ideas and arranging them in a meaningful sequence. This involves the skill of summarizing.

Pacing Technique

A plastic ruler or strip of transparent plastic 5 cm wide is placed vertically down the page to delineate the section of the page where your Pacing Technique will be used. By fixating only the words in the pacing zone, you reduce your reading time by about one half. But you don't reduce your comprehension by one half because you are forced to think beyond the words your eyes are seeing. When your thoughts are on the same subject as the material you are reading, the addition of your personal experience to the reading increases your understanding and memory.

If you read within the pacing zone by sliding back and forth in a Z or S-type pattern to the bottom of the page, you will find that you have read about 200 words with no more than 50 or 60 fixations. All the time you are reading in this way, your eyes are seeing and picking-up the odd word from peripheral vision and you are thinking all the time and putting together ideas, because the mind abhors a vacuum.

The first 10-15 times you use this technique, expect to be frustrated. At first you may remember only three or four words from each reading, but your objective is to go past the literal act of remembering isolated words, to collecting and relating ideas. This takes a lot of practice, so don't give up! Once you have become used to this manner of reading, you can develop the use of the technique further by letting your eyes stray beyond the boundaries of the ruler, selecting from the page the words that are most informative. As you practice in this way, try to fixate on parts of speech, i.e. nouns, verbs, adjectives, etc. You will find that you start to see more and more through peripheral vision, and as a result you will find that you are concentrating more and speeding-up your thinking.

Pacing Exercise

1. Place the book you intend to read in front of you and place the plastic ruler or strip as described above.
2. Use your right index finger or a pen as a pacer, moving it smoothly down the center of the page, over the transparent strip. This may be helpful until you have disciplined your eyes to "pace the page." You may find that moving a 3 x 5 cm card down the plastic strip will be less distracting. The reason to use either the card, a pen, or your fingers in this way is to keep your eyes moving down.
3. When you reach the bottom of the page, jot down any words you remember. If you do not remember any words at all, don't let this upset you - you will improve with practice. Eventually you will remember thoughts and groups of words. By pausing frequently to mentally summarize what you have read, you will organize your thoughts and improve retention.

To acquire the skill of rapid reading requires you to break old habits and form new ones. The most important habit to break is the habit of reading word-by-word, while expecting complete comprehension. Many reading exercises require you to forget comprehension and concentrate all your efforts on the physical skill of fast reading.

To master the Pacing Technique you must understand the training you are going to give your mind. You are being asked to look at words so fast that you cannot possibly pronounce them, and so fast that you cannot understand them either. Every time you do the above exercises you will comprehend a few words. As you continue with these exercises, you will begin to grasp thoughts and eventually, you will read at a much higher rate. When performing this type of exercise, you should always go back and re-read the passage at a comfortable rate, i.e. at a rate at which you can obtain understanding.

Every time you do a speed-exercise and then return to what appears to be your normal speed, you will find that your normal speed has become faster. Since written English is often highly redundant, i.e. much of the material can be omitted without any loss of meaning, a large proportion of information in a text can be absorbed through peripheral vision. Words that are highly likely to occur in a given context do not have to be checked by looking directly at them - peripheral vision can check that they are what is expected even while the eye is fixating elsewhere. The Pacing Technique helps prepare

> Pacing allows you to grasp words faster than you can read or even recognize them.

you to read in this expanded way, reading not along each line, but from side to side of the center of the page, taking in most of a line in one glance, and also peripherally absorbing several further lines beneath it. Making fuller use of peripheral vision, the skilled reader is able to get a better idea of the general sense of what is to follow, and this helps to speed up reading as well as to understand and integrate the material. This is why many students find that as soon as they become adept at speed reading, their comprehension actually increases. They have a broader perspective of what they are reading, and since they are reading faster, the short-term memory for what has just been read goes back several sentences further and the words currently being read are understood within a larger context.

High-speed training has two further advantages: It encourages you to see the key words in the text; and it brings the right hemisphere (which controls peripheral vision) into the reading process, increasing integration and thereby facilitating the right-brain's ability to synthesize relationships within the material.

Scanning

A scan is a fixed pattern of search. Scanning is a useful preliminary action, to preview material rapidly before reading it in-depth. This gives you more of the context of what you go on to read and having viewed it once already, it will have some familiarity and retention will be improved.

1. Make a rapid scan of a light novel. Start at a rate of 15 seconds per page. Later, with practice, this time can be reduced to 12 or 10 seconds per page or even less.
2. You are scanning for significant characters, events and conflicts. At the end of each chapter stop to review what you have just read. Then try and speculate about the contents of the next chapter.
3. When you have scanned several chapters, no more than five, then you will probably need to ask yourself some questions relating to missed events and information, in order to be able to follow the development of the story. Speculate on these answers, then go back and re-read these chapters normally, to see if you were correct.
4. When you have reached the end of the book in the above manner, take some time to summarize the story mentally. Form and answer any unanswered questions about the story and evaluate what you gained from this book. By using the above exercises you will soon find that you have much greater concentration and retention. Through these procedures you will have developed a lasting and very useful skill.

> Scanning allows you to preview material before reading it in depth.

Scanning techniques are not really useful for fiction because you don't want to know what's going to happen ahead of time! With serious, non-fiction material scanning techniques are useful to assess the contents and quality of the work, to provide a context for your study, and to find a particular datum or to decide whether to actually study the material. But it is of little value to be able to read at 2,000 words per minute if half an hour later, 90% of the information has been forgotten. Reading, as described earlier, includes not only the recognition and assimilation of the written material, but also understanding, comprehension, retention, recall and communication.

The most common approach to the study of a new text is the "start and slog" approach. The reader opens the book at page one and reads through to the end. This might seem the most obvious approach, but it is in fact an inefficient use of the reader's knowledge and time and has a number of disadvantages:

1. Time may be wasted going over material that is already familiar, or that is irrelevant to the study in question, or which may be more conveniently summarized later.
2. The reader has no overall perspective until he finishes the text, and possibly not even then.
3. Any information that is retained is usually disorganized; it is seldom well-integrated with the rest of the book nor with the reader's whole body of knowledge.
4. Motivation is low and the reader tends to become bored and tired, leading to poor reading efficiency.

Effective process for In-Depth Reading

A linear approach to study is like going shopping by systematically walking along each street, going into every shop, hoping to find something but not knowing what. The holistic approach to study parallels the normal activity of shopping: one prepares a list of what is required, goes only down the relevant streets (noticing other shop windows on the way in case they contain unexpected items of interest), and visits only those stores that contain all that one needs, with time and energy to spare.

In-Depth Reading or **"Study"** is the most complicated and slowest of the reading processes. After an initial survey or pre-reading (scanning), gathering the context and main concepts, the in-depth reading involves critical and analytical thinking to interpret, evaluate, judge, and reflect on information and ideas. There are four main aspects to in-depth reading:

1. Gathering facts and ideas.
2. Sorting facts and ideas for relative importance and their relationship to one another.
3. Measuring these ideas against one's existing knowledge base.
4. A process of selection, separating the ideas into those that you wish to remember or act upon, and ideas that you wish to reject.

In-depth reading techniques are a form of Self-Questioning. As we read we try to answer questions of HOW and WHY together with the implied suggestions: explain, describe, evaluate, interpret, illustrate, and define. When reading nonfiction and other serious material, the full procedure is as follows:

Establish Purpose

Answer the following question as carefully and completely as possible: What do I want to learn from this material? Your answer to this question is your purpose for reading. It may help at this stage to review your current knowledge of the subject. This increases expectancy of what is to come, and exposes gaps in one's knowledge and a corresponding desire to fill the vacuum.

Survey a Book or Publication

Read the title, any subtitles, jacket summaries (in the case of a book), and identify the source of the publication, i.e. the author and publisher. Read the date of publication or copyright. The book may well have gone beyond its sell-by-date, e.g. a book on electric motors written in 1950 would be irrelevant, unless perhaps you were trying to mend Grandma's lawnmower.

Analyze the Index. The particular concepts listed and the way in which they are organized will tell you a particular author's bias and whether or not the book will cover the ideas that you are trying to get wise on. Frequently, the Index is a better guide for these purposes than the Contents page.

Read the Preface. Nearly always written last, it will often provide an excellent summary, and usually a statement of purpose for the book and a note on the author's perspective on the subject. Also scan the Forward and Introduction.

Read the Table of Contents. Note the sequence and check for chapter summaries. Chapter summaries are an abstract of the chapter contents. They will frequently inform you whether or not a particular publication is suitable for your purposes.

The next step is to look at the visual material. Read the maps, graphs, illustrations, charts, and bold headings.

Get a close feel for the actual contents of the book by looking at the beginnings and ends of chapters, subsection headings, and anything else which catches the eye - bold print, italicized sections, and the like. Read any summaries the author may have provided. If there are study questions at the end of each chapter, you should look at these also. This will give you an indication of the level of the book in relation to your present knowledge.

Once you have completed these steps you can decide to use the book or not.

Revise Purpose

Once you have surveyed the material and gained more information, and assuming you have decided to use the book, then revise your original purpose for reading the book. Ask yourself: Why am I reading this? This will establish your specific learning objectives.

Study in Depth

Keeping in mind what you want to learn, speculate on what the material will tell you. Begin to read with the satisfaction of your objectives in mind. Sometimes it is inappropriate to start at the beginning, so decide where to start reading. Your overall purpose for reading the material is your best guide. Note: the manner in which the author presents his ideas will demand that you constantly vary the rate of reading and the reading technique you are using, if you wish to be efficient. If you continue reading at the same rate for a prolonged period, it is a good indication that you are not reading flexibly and that you are allowing yourself to become inefficient.

Make notes, jot down main ideas and Key Words and use Mind Maps (see later chapters). It also helps to mark or underline key words and concepts in the book itself, with a soft lead pencil that can easily be erased, to aid review. If it is your own book, do not be afraid to use different colored pens; it helps memory and distinguishes different themes and topics. Be prepared to omit sections that are irrelevant, already familiar, padding, repetition, outdated, or excess examples. Also reject false arguments, such as: generalization from the particular; false premises; undefined sources; misuse of statistics, and the like.

> Take notes, identify key words, and use Mind Maps to help you learn.

Continually ask **WHO, WHAT, WHY, HOW, WHERE and WHEN** questions, as an interactive dialogue between yourself and the study material, in order to extract the important facts.

The **Who** question helps you to hold in mind any significant students.

Why classifies purposes.

How classifies cause and effect sequences, time sequences, procedure or process instructions, or where the new information fits into your life.

The **Where** question points to where the action is taking place or where the new information can be used.

The **When** question can both denote when a subject takes place and when you can use the information.

Finally, the **What** question allows you to take a quick survey of your current knowledge.

Ask yourself:

Who

What

Why

How

Where

When

Take regular breaks every thirty or forty minutes. After each short rest break, take a minute to review the previous work: this consolidates the retention.

Evaluation

Your thoughts should be organized in such a way as to describe the things that you have learned that definitely focus on your primary purpose. Your thoughts may be organized in the following way:

- State the most important idea or concept pertaining to your reading purpose.
- List related keywords, facts, and information in order of importance - using as few words as possible - that pertain to your learning objectives.
- Finally, jot down important words or phrases in relation to the ideas listed above. The most important things to jot down are key characters, important events, places, and dates. These will act as thought joggers or memory clues, which relate directly to the primary and secondary ideas listed.

Rapid Reading Techniques

Effective learners use certain reading techniques that greatly increase both their comprehension and the time required to learn new subjects.

The SQ3R Method

As we have already seen, the SQ3R method incorporates the following actions:

- Scan.
- Question.
- Read.
- Review.
- Recite.

Scanning provides a rapid overview. Many well written books follow logical outlines that can orient the reader to the subject matter.

The outline might follow this pattern:

Title.

Table of Contents.

Main Introduction and conclusion.

Chapter 1.

Introduction.

Conclusion.

Chapter 2.

Chapter 3.

Conclusion.

SQ3R stands for:
Scan
Question
Read
Review
Recite

Question

Questioning is a natural, instinctive, second step that most learners follow. In the scanning process, certain questions naturally arise. These should be noted in a short list of questions to be answered through reading. The questioning procedure helps the reader stay focused.

Reading occurs very rapidly if a systematic plan is followed: First, determine the main idea from the title, the first paragraph, and the last paragraph. Second, determine if a large subject is divided into smaller subjects with some outlining scheme. Next, follow the title, introduction, body, conclusion rule to find the main idea of each smaller section. Each smaller section can then be scanned for keywords. Keyword recognition signals the reader to pay closer attention to critical definitions and ideas that follow.

Review as often as necessary to keep focused. Outlining and note taking often help. Reviewing new material on a strict schedule is necessary to solidify new material in the memory, and to transfer it from short term memory to long term memory. Generally memory is lost by one-half for each doubled time increment. One day after first learning one-half is lost. By day two, one-half of that remaining memory is lost, and by day four, one-half again is lost. By day four, only one-sixteenth of the original memory is intact.

By way of comparison, review after one day results in only one-half of the material that was reviewed being lost. If reviewed again on day two, the amount lost is again divided by two. If reviewed six times in a thirty-two day period, the about retained will be more than ninety-eight percent and the amount lost will only be about two per-cent in the next thirty-two days versus fifty per-cent in one day.

Key Word Noting

A lot of students are dissatisfied with their note taking. They realize that they take down too many words, which in turn makes it difficult to get an overview. They find it difficult to sort the essential facts out of a lecture, a meeting or study materials. Very few students have had a satisfactory training in effective note taking, so the purpose of this portion of this book is to improve this skill.

Association plays a dominant role in nearly every mental function, and words themselves are no exception. The brain associates divergently as well as linearly, carrying on thousands of different actions at the same time, searching, sorting and selecting, relating and making synthesis as it goes along, using left and right brain faculties. Thus a person often finds that in conversation, his mind is not just behaving linearly, but racing on in different directions, exploring to create new ideas and evaluating the ramifications of what is being said. Although a single line of words is coming out, a continuing and enormously complex process is taking place in the mind throughout the conversation. At the same time subtle changes in intonation, body position, facial expression, eye language, and so on, are integrated into the overall process.

Similarly the listener or reader is not simply observing a long list of words; he is receiving each word in the context of the ideas and concepts that surround it, and interpreting it in his own unique way, making evaluations and criticisms based upon his prior knowledge, experience and beliefs. You only have to consider a simple word and start recognizing the associations that come into your mind, to see that this is true.

> Key Words are concrete words that encapsulate the meaning of surrounding sentences.

Words that have the greatest associative power may be described as **Key Words**. These are concrete, specific words which encapsulate the meaning of the surrounding sentence or sentences. They generate strong images, and are therefore easier to remember. The important ideas, the words that are most memorable and contain the essence of the sentence or paragraph are the key words. The rest of the words are associated descriptions, grammatical constructions, and emphasis, and this contextual material is generally forgotten within a few seconds, though much of it will come to mind when the key word is reviewed.

Because of their greater meaningful content, key words tend to "lock up" more information in memory and are the "keys" to recalling the associated ideas. The images they generate are richer and have more associations. They are the words that are remembered, and when recalled, they "unlock" the meaning again. When a young child begins to speak, he starts with keywords, especially concrete nouns, stringing them together directly - for example, "Peter ball" or "Anne tired." It is not until later that sentences include grammatical construction, to give expressions such as "Please would you throw me the ball" or "I am feeling tired."

Taking Notes

Taking notes performs the valuable functions of:

- Imposing organization upon the material.
- Allowing associations, inferences and ideas to be jotted down.
- Bringing attention to what is important.
- Enhancing later recall.

Since we do not remember complete sentences, it is a waste of time to write them down. The most effective note taking concentrates on the key words of the lecture or text. In selecting the key words, a person is brought into active contact with the information. The time which would have been spent making long-winded notes can be spent thinking around the concepts. One is not simply copying down in a semi-conscious manner but is becoming aware of the meaning and significance of the ideas, and forming images and associations between them. This increases comprehension and memory. Because the mind is active, concentration is maintained, and review of the notes becomes quick and easy.

The ability to pick out the most appropriate word as a "key" word is vital if you want to remember the most important information from any text. We mainly use the following parts of speech when we pick keywords:

- **Nouns**: identify the name of a person, place or object. They are the most essential information in a text. "Common nouns" are whole classes of students or things, e.g. man, dog, table, sports, ball. "Proper nouns" name a particular person or thing, e.g. Beethoven, the "Emperor" Concerto, Vienna.
- **Verbs**: indicate actions, things that happen, e.g. to bring, kiss, exist, drink, sing.
- **Adjectives**: describe qualities of nouns (students and other things) - how they appear or behave, e.g. old, tall, foolish, beautiful.
- **Adverbs**: indicate how a verb (activity) is applied, e.g. gently, fully, badly.

A key word or phrase is one which funnels into itself a range of ideas and images from the surrounding text, and which, when triggered, funnels back the same information. It will tend to be a strong noun or verb, on occasion accompanied by an additional key adjective or adverb. Nouns are the most useful as key words, but this does not mean you should exclude other words. Key words are simply words that give you the **most inclusive concept**. They do not have to be actual words used in the text - you may have a better word that encapsulates and evokes the required associations, and a phrase may be necessary rather than just a word.

The more that notes consist of key words, the more useful they are and the better they are remembered. Ideally, notes should be based upon key words and accompanying key images, and incorporate summary diagrams and illustrative drawings.

Associative Networks

Memory is not recorded like a tape recording, with each idea linked to the next in a continuous stream; instead, the information is recorded in large interconnecting associative networks. Concepts and images are related in various ways to numerous other points in the mental network. The act of encoding an event, i.e. memorizing, is simply that of forming new links in the network, i.e. making new associations. Subconsciously, the mind will continue to work on the network, adding further connections which remain implicit until they are explicitly recognized, i.e. they enter the pre-conscious as relevant material, and are picked up by the spotlight of consciousness. Such associative networks explain the incredible versatility and flexibility of human information processing. Memory is not like a container that gradually fills up, it is more like a tree growing hooks onto which the memories are hung. So the capacity of memory keeps growing - the more you know, the more you can know. There is no practical limit to this expansion because of the phenomenal capacity of the neuronal system of the brain, which in most students is largely untapped, even after a lifetime of mental processing.

Mind Maps

Meaning is an essential part of all thought processes, and it is meaning that gives order to experience. Indeed the process of perception is ultimately one of extracting meaning from the environment. If the mind is not attending, information will go "in one ear and out the other;" the trace it leaves may well be too weak to be recalled in normal circumstances.

If concentration is applied, i.e. there is conscious involvement with the information, more meaning is extracted, more meaningful connections are made with existing understanding, the memory is stronger, and there will be more opportunity to make meaningful connections with new material in the future.

Because the brain naturally organizes information in associative networks, it makes sense to record notes about information you want to remember in a similar way. Using the method of Mind Maps, all the various factors that enhance recall have been brought together, in order to produce a much more effective system of note taking. A mind map works organically in the same way as the brain itself, so it is therefore an excellent interface between the brain and the spoken or written word.

Paradoxically, one of the greatest advantages of **Mind Maps** is that they are seldom needed again once formed. The very act of constructing a map is so effective in fixing ideas in memory that very often a whole Mind Map can be recalled without going back to it at all. Because it is so strongly visual, frequently it can be simply reconstructed in the 'mind's eye'.

To make a Mind Map, one starts at the center of a new sheet of paper, writing down the central theme very boldly, preferably in the form of a strong visual image, so that everything in the map is associated with it. Then work outwards in all directions, adding branches for each new concept, and further small branches and twigs for associated ideas as they occur. In this way one produces a growing and organized structure composed of key words and key images (see the previous section on "Key Words").

Two vertical lines

If you use a glass "anti-glare" screen, draw two vertical lines in felt-tip, 5 cm. apart, so that you have a strip 5 cm. wide located over the middle of the text you are reading.

A Mind Map visually links words and ideas to a central theme.

Now move your eyes in a 'Z' pattern down this central strip, at a speed slightly faster than is comfortable. Because your mind is not reading each word, it is forced to 'fill in the gaps'. This engages much more of the mind, since it has to build associations and patterns in the written material. This in turn leads to greater comprehension and increased memory of what was read. This technique takes advantage of the fact that much of written English is highly redundant; a lot of words can be skipped without any loss of meaning.

Strips reading

Cut the text you are reading into three perpendicular strips. Place the pieces before yourself. Make the one-inch blanks between the strips. Read quickly. The higher the speed of reading the higher the level of understanding. Soon you will not notice the space between the strips. Shift the central strip in any order, creating maximum inconvenience for the brain. Let the brain work. Now place the strips back in their initial order. Read the text. What do you feel?

Read first sentence

Since often the first sentence of each paragraph states the main idea of that paragraph, while the other sentences elaborate on that idea, you can skim read by just reading the first sentences. In some cases, you can get enough information by only reading the first sentence in each paragraph.

Unfortunately, some writers make their paragraphs so long, that they have several ideas in them, and others stick the important sentences in the middle. In such cases, you can't use the first sentence method effectively.

Browse through the publication - forward or backward - so that you get to know what's in it and where it's located. Notice the layout and how the information is presented. Notice the table of contents and any special sections. Don't be too serious - it's best to be playful.

Notice which sections pique your interest, but don't read them yet. Catch titles, subtitles, pictures, and charts. When you find something interesting, think of how you can use it - reading for information should be a goal-seeking activity. Decide how much time you can afford, and then go for it.

Follow these tips and your reading will become purposeful, active, questioning and goal oriented. This means you save time and get more information from the time you spend reading!

Active reading

When you are reading a document in detail, it often helps if you highlight, underline and annotate it as you go on. This emphasizes information in your mind, and helps you to review important points later.

Doing this also helps to keep your mind focused on the material and stops it from wandering.

This is obviously only something to do if you own the document! If you find that active reading helps, then it may be worth photocopying information in more expensive texts. You can then read and mark the photocopies.

If you are worried about destroying the material, ask yourself how much your investment of time is worth. If the benefit you get by active reading reasonably exceeds the value of the book, then the book is disposable.

Think for a moment, what you read

You were taught to read with your tongue because you were taught to read by being taught to speak the words. Want to enjoy what you read? Think for a moment - what were the best books you've ever read in your life? The ones you enjoyed the most? I'm going to bet they were the best books for you because your imagination was totally engrossed in the book. Thus your brain was working at a much higher capacity than when you aren't using your imagination.

Breathing and reading

Breathing is also a good way to improve the rate at which you read. Try to take solid, deep breaths instead of short quick breaths. This will allow you to calm down and try to read with more concentration.

Reading for SSAT

All of the exercises and theory presented above will greatly enhance your reading speed and accuracy for the SSAT.

How important is the RC section?

At the end of the day, SSAT RC, despite its question types, word games, and close answer choices, is about understanding what one reads! So in theory, if you are clever enough to understand everything you read you should get all RC questions correct!

Yet, typically, students who think RC is easy, make many mistakes in this section. The RC section is a bit sneaky and you may not feel as though you are making mistakes.

RC also carries a huge importance for the timing in verbal section. If you plan to solve an RC within five minutes, consider that the time doubles immediately when you don't understand the material, because you need to spend another five minutes re-reading the passage.

Winning Tips for SSAT Reading Comprehension

What is the most effective reading method for SSAT?

Exploratory reading method is probably the most effective method to tackle SSAT RC. Exploratory reading is the half-way point between skimming and close reading, and it's similar to pleasure reading. You want to acquaint yourself with the subject, but you do not need complete understanding and retention. Perhaps you are reading supplementary material that you will not be held accountable for, or perhaps you only need to gain general knowledge from a text that will be available if you need to look up specific references. In exploratory reading, read as quickly as possible. Keep your mind on the material. Upon finishing each section of the material, pause to rest the eyes. See if you can summarize what you have just read. The ability to summarize is another skill that can be developed only by practice.

Try to read the whole text of the passage once, if possible. Many people think you should just skim the passage or read the first lines of each paragraph, and not to read the passage. We believe this is an error. If you misunderstand the main idea of the passage, you will certainly get at least some of the questions wrong.

> Exploratory Reading allows you to familiarize yourself with a passage, but doesn't require complete comprehension.

For improved RC, you need to focus on the main idea of the article, rather than details. Try to focus on what the author is trying to tell you, what the main points of the article are, as well as the logical relationship between paragraphs.

When you read the article, imagine yourself walking in a new department store. You need to remember where all the major product categories are, and not all the locations of thousands of items. Only if you have a high level mental map of where things are, can you find a specific item in the shortest time. RC is the same, you get the gist of what an article or passage is about, for the author's main points (what she/he is trying to tell you), and the functions of each passage. Then you can easily answer most of the questions, and if there are detail questions (normally there is only one or none per article), then you can go back to the right section and read it again to get the answer correctly in the shortest time.

Exploratory Reading combined with the reading techniques below should result in a much better performance on the RC section:

- **Start to read SLOWLY.** This is crucial. Because most students are so nervous and conscious of time, they start the passage with a blitz. This is totally counterproductive. You MUST start reading slowly and make sure you understand the overall issue, key arguments, who the players are, and the like.
- **Paraphrase with exaggeration!** This technique can be very effective, especially if you combine it with the Visual Reading Technique discussed earlier. You should think for one to two seconds in every two to three sentences and repeat your understanding in your own language. But when you paraphrase, add something to it. When you repeat your understanding in your own language, say something in your mind that will make you remember it. For example, if the author says scientist A was wrong. I paraphrase this in my own language: Wow look at this author, he says this stupid scientist made wrong assumptions. Let's see why.... It may sound silly but it is very effective. This exaggeration also keeps your attention at high levels. If you can also visualize this exaggeration, there is no way you will get a question wrong.
- **Read with the desire to learn and at least agree or disagree with the author!** In almost all passages, either the author or the people mentioned argue for X and some other people argue for Y, or there are two things described and author gives evidence and arguments for each. You should try to take sides when possible, and criticize either the author or the other party. This technique will help you follow turns in the passage, evaluate evidence and claims, and anticipate what might come next. **So, simply stated, take sides.** Even in a neutral passage that just describes a phenomenon, you can find a way to stay focused by using exaggeration and visualization. Never ever read a SSAT passage as if you are reading a magazine.
- Remember that the tone or attitude of the passage is usually respectful and moderate, never going to extremes of praise or criticism. So the tone of the articles, even when there is criticism in the passage toward an academic or her work, is always balanced

and moderate. In the same vein, articles that deal with minorities or ethnic groups are almost always positive and sympathetic.

Look out for **structural words** that tell you the important ideas or transitions in a passage. The following is a non-exhaustive list of such structural words, categorized by type:

- Continue the Idea Words
    - Similarly
    - Moreover
    - Additionally
    - In the same way
    - Likewise
- Conclusion Words
    - Thus
    - Therefore
    - Hence
    - So
    - In summary
    - In conclusion
- Contradiction or Contrast Words
    - Nevertheless
    - Nonetheless
    - However
    - But
    - Although
    - Though
    - Even though
    - Notwithstanding
    - Yet
    - Despite
    - In spite of
    - On the one hand...on the other hand

- While
- Unlike

Recap before going on to the answers: The most common mistake that students make is that they rush to the questions immediately after reading the passage. I hear you say "What on earth should I do otherwise?" Well, here it is: take a few seconds, scroll up, and just remember what you just read in one to two words per paragraph and visualize the flow of the passage for the last time.

Understand definitions of author's tone. Is it tentative, a wholehearted endorsement, skeptical, approving?

Go back to the text of the passage for the answers. Many test-takers fail to return to the text of the passage to look for the correct answers. They rely solely on their memories and understanding of the passage after having read or skimmed it. Wrong. ETS is counting on that. Go back to the text to look for information to answer the questions. Nine times out of ten, the answer lies within the passage.

How to deal with difficult passages

Difficulty is not directly linked to the length, structure, or topic of the passage. You can have a long and convoluted passage, but with simple questions, or a short and easy article, but with answers so close you need to read the passage five times! There are several ways in which an RC can become tough:

a) Multiple dimension passages: Who-What-Where-How-Why?

These are passages that present you with two or three theories, items, or events at the same time. So far so good, but then the passage talks about two to three attributes of each of these two to three main things. So you might have a bug that can fly but cannot walk, then you might have a bug that can walk but cannot fly, then the first group can have members that are red but die at a young age, whereas others are in different colors but die old. The second group might have members which have a thick shell in red and reproduce young, the other group's members may have no shell and reproduce when they are old, and so on.

The passage overloads you with similar but different information relating to all the main things (bugs, events, people, theories, etc.) in the passage. Most people would say there is no need to understand those details; I say it is very important to understand the main differences between these groups as you read the passage. Not understanding these details in these sections is a fatal mistake.

How Winners tackle these kind of passages:

- Identify points of difference (how do they differ) and also parity (how they are similar) between these different things. Is it the time they die? Is it whether they have a shell? Is it their color?
- Depending on the situation, write down the main points and try to understand where the author focuses and gives examples. Then paraphrase your understanding (again using exaggeration).
- While it is correct that in RC you don't need to read all the details, not all details are nonsense. If author gives details to prove his case or to explain an issue, try to get a good idea of where in the passage the details are in case you need to come back to them.

b) Close Answers

Sometimes the passage itself will be easy to read, as is likely with respect to passages on business or social sciences and the like, and since the passage is easy you will relax and your attention level will drop. Then, when you start reading the questions you will find that the answers are so close, you simply cannot decide which is the correct one.

When you get these passages, understanding the passage is not enough. No matter how carefully you read the passage or how effectively you take notes, you will have to evaluate at least two, and probably three answer choices. They will be very close. To trick you even more, SSAT will make the two choices as follows:

a. Half of this choice will be exactly true and will be put in a very good format. So if the author described a book, half of this choice will say, author described a book! So you will say: Oh this is 100% true so this might be the answer. Yet the other part will be blurry, it will use words from the passage. Your brain will remember those words and also the halo effect created by the first half (which is crystal clear and correct) will make you think this is the answer.

b. This answer choice will not be so crystal clear, maybe it will say that the author introduces an issue and give examples. This part will be okay but still not as good as the first part of the answer choice a). Then, the second part will be even less appealing but you won't think it is incorrect, you will feel it is just not that direct and "good looking" as the answer choice a).

In difficult passages you will always face this dilemma: **YOU HAVE TO LEARN HOW TO CHOOSE THE RIGHT ANSWER WHEN YOU HAVE TWO CLOSE ANSWER CHOICES AS DESCRIBED ABOVE!** SSAT knows that your brain will remember a few words from the passage and also that you will prefer more direct and "good looking" answer. In the above example, answer choice a) will be wrong because one word or one part will be wrong. What do you do? Typically, if you know you have been doing fairly well, and if you get a passage that is easy to read, this implies that the answer choices will be close!

Spend less time reading the passage. **You will need time when answering.** Then, when answering questions, write on a piece of paper the choices that you can eliminate until you have only two choices left. Then use the process of elimination by focusing on single words rather than on the complete answers.

Ask yourself: IS THIS REALLY TRUE? If answer says " the author questioned the validity of a theory," directly ask yourself if the author really did that. If the answer is "no," then one word in the answer is wrong and thus the whole thing is wrong.

Remember this rule: if one piece of information, such as a verb used to describe an idea, event, etc. is wrong, then the entire answer choice will be wrong. It doesn't matter whether the rest, which might be 90% of the answer choice is correct and very nicely put. One word wrong=>GONE.

Typically, business passages, social sciences passages, and the like are easy to read and will definitely have close answer choices. Don't relax when you read these passages if you want to nail the next four questions! In your prep, try to solve business and social science passages as well - don't just focus on science passages. Remember, the topic does not make a passage easy or tough.

C) Satiric/Unclear Tones

Just a short piece of advice: sometimes an author will use satire or will write in such a way as to disguise his tone - you won't be able to understand what he really thinks. Normally, understanding should be easy. Still, if you notice the author is using a satirical or unclear tone and you don't really understand what he thinks, STOP READING! UNDERSTAND WHAT IS GOING ON. FIGURE OUT WHO THINKS WHAT. THEN MOVE ON. NEVER, EVER READ THE WHOLE THING WITHOUT FIRST UNDERSTANDING THE POSITION OF THE AUTHOR (assuming he or she has stated one).

If you feel like none of the answer makes sense, there could be a couple of factors at work:

- You are not reading the question right. You are misinterpreting the question or the answer choices.
- Your interpretation of the relevant part of the passage is wrong.

Close your eyes, take a deep breath, and look at the question with a fresh mind. DO NOT STARE AT THE QUESTION for minutes; you won't get it if you are looking at it from the wrong angle. DON'T PANIC. There is nothing that is impossible to do on the SSAT. It is just a matter of understanding what you read. You can surely crack it, just stay cool.

If you feel like there are too many correct answers, a couple of factors could be at work:

- You understood the question and passage correctly but you fail to notice the minor differences among choices. FOCUS ON WORDS - COMPARE THE MEANING OF CHOICES WORD BY WORD!
- Sometimes everything really depends on the meaning of one or two words. When you face a dilemma between two choices, treat it as a SC question, focus on the differences between choices, and if necessary write down the main verbs, etc.

Noticing shifts in Passages

PAY ATTENTION TO THE PASSAGES YOU ARE READING. BE ALERTED WHEN YOU SEE:

- **A comparison**. Japan is ....yet most of other Asian countries....
  The comparison may be more subtle. Just keep your eyes open.
- **What others think about X** (author, thing, book, research, findings). RCs are all about opinions! Always understand the opinions mentioned in the passage. OPINIONS AND POSITIONS ARE KEY TO SOLVING MOST PASSAGES.
- The **WHYs.** If the author talks about something and then he gives **REASONS** for a position, belief, etc. or he talks about an event and gives **REASONS, YOU HAVE TO REMEMBER THESE WHYS, or where to find them if required.**
- **Examples/Analogies/Interesting stuff:** If the author starts to explain an issue and gives examples, uses analogies, or talks about something striking, open your eyes. You will get a question from that portion of the passage.

The top 3 reasons why students get questions wrong:

- Deceptive answers. Most of these contain actual words or phrases from the passage. Be especially suspicious when the question asks you to "infer" the answer.
- "Half-truths". Ensure that the whole answer is right - not just a part of it. A classic example is "Author is resigned but hopeful." If you feel the author is just resigned but never hopeful then this answer is *wrong*. Don't pick it because it "sounds" right.
- Extreme language. Avoid words like - ALL, NEVER, and ALWAYS. They almost always signal a wrong choice. Go for more generic and accommodating answer choices.

Using the 80 - 20 rule to your advantage

Deceptive Answers, Half-Truths, and Extreme Language trick many who take the SSAT into choosing an incorrect answer.

What does 80% comprehension mean? That you understand 80% of the words you read? 80% of the concepts? 80% of the sentences? That you could repeat back 80% of the words?

Get 80% of the information in 20% of the time by simply reading the title, subtitle, bold type, last paragraph, and first paragraph - spend only 30-45 seconds. Then reflect on the relevance of the information for you. If it is important to read more, go to the next step. Otherwise, find another article.

Take one to two minutes to skim through the article to find the core idea. Know what is being expressed. Do you need more details? Know where to find them.

Read lightly and flexibly. Know what you need. Since very few words carry the meaning, speed up to pass redundant or useless information.

How to get a hyper focus on the SSAT

Getting into a **hyper focused** and relaxed state isn't as hard as you might think, and simply requires following some very basic steps. As you progress with speed-reading skills, you will be able to pare down the steps and get yourself into this state in a matter of thirty seconds.

In order to succeed at anything, it is necessary to remove all self-doubt and to cast aside any inhibitive preconceived notions you might have about the task and your ability. Think of all those negative feelings you have about reading. For example, you might feel that reading is boring, that you have trouble retaining the information you read about, that you take too long to get through a single chapter, and so on. Mentally rake up all these assumptions you have (as if they were autumn leaves) and picture putting them in a plastic bag. Tie a knot in the bag and fling it off a cliff - watch this bag of junk sail away into nothingness.

Think positively about what you are about to do. Think, "this is great...I am going to learn to focus and to zip through reams of reading material. This is a skill that I can learn and I will learn." Your mind has a very large capacity to learn and you can definitely learn to read quickly and effectively. Imagine how much you are going to learn and how much time you will save with this new skill. Remember that limitations are self-imposed and as soon as you say "I can," well, you probably can! Believe in human brain.

Sit up straight. **Posture** is very important to fast reading, if you're slouched, your mind will be "lazy" and inattentive.

Next, it is important to become physically relaxed. Top athletes often describe feeling loose and relaxed before the best performances of their lives. The same holds for brain activity. To learn and to absorb information properly, being calm, loose, and relaxed is imperative. To get into this super zone, close your eyes and transport yourself to a serene place. Perhaps you are walking through deep woods. Just pick a personal paradise and go there mentally. Use free imagination. Breathe deeply through the nose, from your lower abdomen (this is real deep breathing, using your entire diaphragm, and not just the top part). Perhaps you are lying in the grass on your parent's back lawn, face turned to the sun. Perhaps you are sitting at the edge of a calm lake, toes dipped into the warm water. Breathe in and count three long seconds, breathe out and count three long seconds. Do this ten times. Soon you will be able to condense this process and get into the mode by taking a few deep breaths.

Be an active reader

Before you even look at the text, and as you scan it and read it, ask these questions: "What am I going to learn here? What is the author's conclusion? How does the author present the topic? What are the key points to the argument?" Such questions (they should be tailor-made to the type of reading you are doing, and the reason for which you are doing it) function to engage you in the activity. If you ask a question in a lecture, you always remember the answer to the question. Similarly, if you become an "active reader" you are much more likely to retain the information that you amass.

Developing Effective Reading Skills for the SSAT

The SSAT is all about understanding what you read. Understanding a text means extracting the required information from it as efficiently as possible. This also means using different strategies and skills to find out what you are looking for. The following flow chart illustrates how you should approach reading and answering questions for the SSAT:

→ *Reading*

→ *`Making hypotheses about content and function*

→ *Anticipation of where to look for confirmation of the Hypotheses according to what one knows*

→ *Predicting*

→ *Skimming*

→ *Scanning*

→ *Confirmation of one's guess*

→ *Attempting the question*

Reading is a constant process of guessing, predicting and anticipating information.

Aspects of reading - in the context of the SSAT

Concentration and active reading

As a good reader, you should have a purpose and the intention to concentrate. The intention to concentrate is often not enough and you should make concentration possible by reading actively. Read for the meaning behind the words and use your existing knowledge. To concentrate properly you should be as active and spontaneous as you would be in a conversation or discussion. You are allowed to question - in your mind - the propositions put forth, agree with certain points and contribute to those points as you would while having a conversation. While contributing, you will be using your own knowledge .

You have to be careful though. You may tend to go beyond the scope of the discussion and make unnecessary assumptions. Hence, you must make a careful effort to remain within the movement of the author's thought.

Functional reading

The reading that you have to do for the SSAT is very unlike to your casual reading. It is functional reading - reading done with the purpose of assimilating information. You will need every bit of concentration you are capable of. You will have to do your best to cooperate with the author to understand what he wishes to convey.

Looking for information

Your main job is to look for information. Functional reading helps to gather information. Information might consist of:

- Concrete detail, such as numerical facts, sequences of events over a period of time; or
- Impressions or feelings, which may be implicit, expressed clearly, or vaguely hinted at .

You need to cultivate an eye for concrete detail. Most of the questions directed at you will be designed to find out if you can grasp facts clearly. Learn to distinguish between facts and opinions.

When should you take notes?

Functional Reading is done for the purpose of assimilating information.

Note making by drawing diagrams will help you to visualize the information contained in a text. It will help you see at once the main points of the text and how they are related. Don't think drawing a small table in twenty seconds will cost you more time than not taking notes! At the risk of over generalizing, it can be said that if you don't fully understand the What, Where, How, and Why aspects of these tough passages, you will be literally guessing. It is best to draw a simple table for these kind of questions.

Directions : Read the following passage and capture the information in the form of a tree diagram.

We shall outline the four major subfields of anthropology that have emerged in the twentieth century: physical anthropology; archaeology; linguistics; and cultural anthropology.

Physical anthropology deals with human biology across space and time. It is divided into two areas: paleontology, the study of the fossil evidence of primate (including human) evolution; and neonatology, the comparative biology of living primates, including population and molecular genetics, body shapes (morphology), and the extent to which behavior is biologically programmed.

Archaeology is the systematic retrieval and analysis of the physical remains left behind by human beings, including both their skeletal and cultural remains. Both classical civilizations and prehistoric groups, including our pre human ancestors, are investigated.

Linguistics is the study of language across space and time. Historical linguistic attempts to trace the tree of linguistic evolution and to reconstruct ancestral language forms. Comparative (or structural) linguistic attempts to describe formally the basic elements of languages and the rules by which they are ordered into intelligible speech.

Cultural anthropology includes many different perspectives and specialized sub disciplines, but is concerned primarily with describing the forms of social organization and the cultural systems of human groups. In technical usage, ethnography is the description of the social and cultural systems of one particular group, whereas ethnology is the comparison of such descriptions for the purpose of generalizing about the nature of all human groups .

The words to be used in the notes are ethnology, archaeology, structural linguistics, physical anthropology, neonatology, anthropology, historical linguistics, cultural anthropology, linguistic paleontology, and ethnography.

EXPLANATION

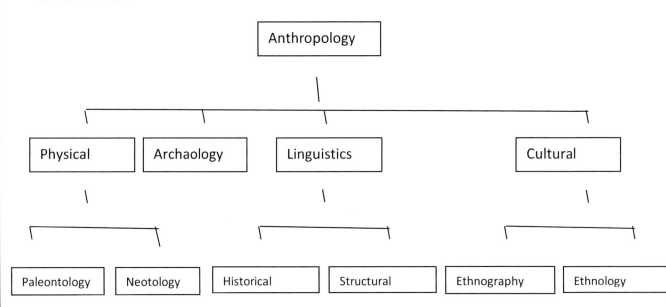

Types of Passages on the SSAT

There are various types of passages that you can get on the SSAT. The following is a broad classification and serves, at best, as an indication of the various types of passages that you could be exposed to when taking the SSAT:

- **Data driven passages.** These enumerate, more often than not, many facts and figures. They can be read perfunctorily, especially if the questions tend to be very specific as to the facts and figures. They are unambiguous and fairly easy to read. While answering the questions one can usually identify the questioned areas very easily. These passages can be gone through quickly even if they are long.

- **Descriptive Passages.** There is a blurred line of difference between this kind of passage and a data driven passage. These passages could describe a situation, e.g. a case-study, or they could describe a place, a scientific phenomenon, an economic situation, etc. They are passages that are invariably read by all of you, at some time or the other. More often than not, you are likely to be comfortable with such passages.

- **Analytical /abstract/abstruse passages.** These passages could be an analysis of a subject/theory (scientific, political or philosophical) or a comparison between two situations/theories. They usually follow a certain pattern: starting with stating the issue being discussed and then going on to critically analyze its plus/minus points. Some others may draw out differences between the two theories and analyze their individual contributions to the relevant body of knowledge as a whole. In these passages, you need to look for the key statements that sum up the nature of the issue, the arguments for/against the issue and the conclusion reached. If you can practice doing this, it will greatly increase your speed and accuracy while tackling such passages.

Some other passages relate to what is called alternative writing: fantasy, philosophy, or theology. Passages about religion, philosophical principles, alternative socio-political writings and the like are examples of such passages. These are fairly difficult to get used to, since the style of writing and the language used is unfamiliar to many of us. These passages are usually dense with ideas, and hence even if they are short, they take longer to read and assimilate .

You have to keep in mind that an abstract passage is not always considered abstract purely on the basis of the subject matter. The style of writing, the thoughts expressed, and the analysis provided are also the parameters by which a passage could be pegged as abstract or abstruse. Hence, please do not have a closed mind about subject matter in passage. The passages may not turn out to be as complex as you imagine them to be.

By and large, students find that factual passages are easier to negotiate than analytical or abstract passages. This is mainly because of two reasons:

- Firstly, the ideas expressed in factual passages tend to deal with real-life and current situations, whereas the ideas in abstract passages are multi-dimensional. They are opinions or beliefs, and cannot be understood in a black-or-white manner. Students find it difficult to relate to such passages, since the questions in these cases tend to be inferential or indirect.

> Explicit questions are based on facts from the passage. Implicit questions require greater understanding.

- Secondly, not many students, in a general way, read abstruse material, unless they are specifically interested, whereas factual and analytical passages are read widely in order to gain knowledge about current happenings.

It follows from the above that **you would need to vary speed with the nature of the material and the kind of writing, keeping in mind the types of questions asked**. Here we use the analogy of eating. There are certain foods one needs to chew for some time before swallowing (pizzas); then again there are others that can be gulped down in a second (milkshakes). Likewise, there are some passages that can be gulped down (understood) quickly. There are others that need a lot more chewing (analyzing/understanding) to be done and therefore you need to spend more time on them. By the same logic, direct questions, more often than not, require less deliberation than questions that are inferential, and hence can be dealt with faster.

As noted earlier, it is important to read a wide variety of material so that you are comfortable with as many types of passages as possible .

Topics for the reading comprehension passages are usually taken from the

1. **Social sciences:** Economics; psychology; sociology; business; history; political science; contemporary issues; etc.
2. **Natural science:** Physics; chemistry; biology; medicine; geography; natural phenomena; astronomy; etc. .
3. **Humanities:** Literature; criticism; art; philosophy; aesthetics; etc.

Question Types & Strategies for tackling them

There are broadly two types of questions - explicit and implicit (or inferential).

Explicit questions are based on facts from the passage. However, the questions in themselves may be trickily worded to confuse the student.

Implicit questions need a greater understanding of the passage, as opposed to direct questions, which may be answered by going back to the text. With inferential questions, unless one understands the author's stance on the general flow of the passage, it becomes difficult for one to answer the questions .

Of the six most important types of questions for Reading Comprehension, we will first look at Main Idea/Primary Purpose Questions, and the strategies we can use to answer them.

Main Idea/Primary Purpose Questions

Many people believe there is no difference between the main or central idea of the passage and the primary purpose of the author of the passage. This is simply not true. Let's take a look at the subtle but important difference between them:

Main Idea

A "main idea" question might look something like one of these:

"Which of the following best states the central idea of the passage?"
"Which of the following most accurately states the main idea of the passage?"
"Which of the following is the principal topic of the passage?"
"The main topic of the passage is...."

Primary Purpose

The question might look like this:

A "primary purpose" question might look like one of these:

"The primary purpose of this passage is to..."

"The primary purpose of the passage as a whole is to..."

"The primary focus of this passage is on which of the following?"

"The main concern of the passage is to..."

"In the passage, the author is primarily interested in...."

"The passage is chiefly concerned with..."

Strategies

Main Idea: Look in the first and last paragraphs for the main idea. Any **conclusion words** like *therefore, thus, so, hence*, etc. that you see are most likely introducing the main idea. The correct answer will say the same thing as it says in the text, but using different words. The Main Idea is not always stated explicitly in the passage – in fact, more likely than not, it is not stated explicitly. Therefore, in order to answer this type of question when the statement of the main idea is more implicit, re-read the first line of every passage, and the last line of the first and last paragraphs. This should give you the general structure or outline of the argument with which you can answer the Main Idea question.

After determining the general structure or content of the argument, eliminate answer choices that are too broad or too specific (i.e. answer choices that go beyond the content of the passage, or that deal with content only discussed in one paragraph of the passage.) Make brief notes – a couple of words - regarding the Main Idea on the text on your scrap paper while you read.

Primary Purpose: What is the author trying to do? What is his intention? If he is evaluating a theory, then the answer could be something like "Discuss an interpretation." Note that the correct answer would deal with "*an* interpretation," because the author is only dealing with **one** theory. If the Primary Purpose is to criticize two new books, then his intention or his primary purpose might be to "Critique new studies." Again, as in Main Idea questions, re-read the *first line* of every passage, and the *last line* of the *first* and *last* paragraphs. This should give you the general structure or outline of the argument, with which you can answer the Primary Purpose question.

Note: A good main idea or primary purpose does not go beyond the scope of the passage, nor does it limit itself to discussing only one part of the passage.

Title Questions

Title questions are very similar to Main Idea questions, though they are less common. Though some of the example passages we use in this tutorial and in the Practice Section are from the New Scientist, and therefore have titles. The passages in the real SSAT will not have titles. A Title question might look like this:

"Which of the following titles best summarizes the passage as a whole?"

Strategy

Treat this as a Main Idea question. A good title sums up the central idea of a passage. Therefore, in order to answer this type of question, do the following:

Look in the first and last paragraphs for the main idea. Any conclusion words like therefore, thus, so, hence, etc. that you see are most likely introducing the Main Idea/Title. The correct answer will say the same thing as it says in the text, but using different words.

Re-read the first line of every passage, and the last line of the first and last paragraphs. This should give you the general structure or outline of the argument, with which you can answer the Title question.

Make brief notes – a couple of words- regarding the Title on the text on your scrap paper while you read.

After determining the general structure or content of the argument, eliminate answer choices that are too broad or too specific, i.e. answer choices that go beyond the content of the passage, or that deal with content only discussed in one paragraph of the passage.

Specific Detail or Target questions

These are probably the most common types of questions, and the easiest to answer. The questions might look like these:

"According to the passage,...."
"The passage states that ...."

Strategy

The Specific Detail or Target that we are looking for could be a Line Number, Name, or Date. Go to the Line Number, Name, or Date and then read several lines above and below it. Find the answer choice that basically says the same thing as in the passage, though usually with different words or word order.

Inference Type Questions

These are probably the most difficult type of Reading Comprehension problem. The questions might look like these:

"It can be inferred that the author makes which of the following assumptions?"
"Which is an assumption underlying the last sentence of the passage?"
"Which of the following, if true, would most strengthen the hypothesis mentioned in lines 17-19?"
"With which of the following statements regarding chaos theory would the author be most likely to agree?"

Strategy

First, treat this type of problem as a Specific Target question. Look for a target in the question, find it in the text, and then look above and below it. Often you do not have to *infer* very much, the answer remains within the text.

If the answer must be inferred and is not stated explicitly within the text, then choose the answer choice that can be inferred or assumed from the information given. Again, you should not have to infer very much – only one or two logical steps removed from the information in the passage.

Make sure that the answer choice you decide on does not violate or contradict the Main Idea of the passage - if it does, the answer choice is probably wrong.

Attitude Questions

Attitude questions might look like these:

"The author's attitude towards Morgan's theory could best be described as one of ..."

Strategy

Look for descriptive words, adjectives or adverbs, that could tell you the author's attitude. For example, the words *unfortunately* or *flaw* suggest a negative connotation, while *strength* or *valuable* emphasize the positive. Make brief notes – a couple of words- regarding the Tone of the text on your scrap paper while you read. Additionally, keep in mind that the author's attitude toward a theory, book, or ethnic group will almost always be respectful, even when somewhat critical.

Structure Questions

Structure questions might look like these:

"Which of the following best describes the organization of the passage?"
"Which of the following best describes the organization of the first paragraph of the passage?"
"One function of the third paragraph is to...."

Strategy

Re-read the *first line* of every passage, and the *last line* of the *first* and *last* paragraphs. This should give you the general structure or outline of the argument, with which you can answer the question. Remember to make brief notes about the structure of the text on your scrap paper. If you are looking for the organization of one paragraph, read the first and second sentence of the paragraph. That will give you a rough idea of what is the structure or organization of the paragraph.

Now that you have absorbed the various techniques and strategies, let us try some RC exercises.

SSAT Reading Comprehension Practice

Passage SET 1

Passage 1

Two theories have often been used to explain ancient and modern tragedy. Each explains important elements of tragedy but, because their conclusions are contradictory, they represent extreme views. The first theory states that all tragedy exhibits the workings of external fate. Most tragedies do leave us with a sense of the supremacy of impersonal power and of the limitation of human effort. But this theory is oversimplified, primarily because it does not acknowledge that fate, as conceived in ancient Greek tragedy, is the internal balancing condition of life. It is external only after the balance has been violated.

The second theory of tragedy states that the act that initiates the tragic process must violate human or divine law. Again it is true that most tragic heroes possess hubris, a kind of pride that makes the hero's downfall morally explicable. But hubris only precipitates catastrophe, just as in comedy the cause of the happy ending is usually some act of humility. This theory of tragedy as morally explicable runs into the question of whether an innocent sufferer is a tragic figure. They are, of course, although it is hard to find moral flaws in them. Cordelia shows sincerity and high spirit in refusing to flatter her father, and Cordelia is hanged. Tragedy, in short, cannot be reduced to the opposition between human effort and external fate, just as it cannot be reduced to the opposition between good and evil.

1.   The primary purpose of the passage is to

    (A) compare and criticize two theories of tragedy.
    (B) develop a new theory of tragedy.
    (C) summarize the thematic content of tragedy.
    (D) reject one theory of tragedy and offer another theory in its place.
    (E) distinguish between tragedy and irony.

2.   The author states that the theories discussed in the passage "represent extreme views" because their conclusions are

(A) unpopular

(B) complex

(C) paradoxical

(D) contradictory

(E) imaginative

3. Which of the following best describes the tone of the passage?

(A) dismissive

(B) ironic

(C) objective

(D) angry

(E) worried

4. The author discusses the role of hubris in tragedy in order to

(A) prove that hubris initiates the tragic process.

(B) establish a criterion that allows a distinction to be made between hubris and sin.

(C) counter the argument that violation of law sets the tragic process in motion.

(D) introduce the concept of external fate as the cause of tragic action.

(E) argue that the theme of omnipotent external fate is shared by comedy and tragedy.

5. According to the author, Cordelia is an example of a figure who

(A) transcended both the laws of fate and the laws of society.

(B) sinned, but whose sin did not set the tragic process in motion.

(C) disobeyed a moral law, but was not punished for doing so.

(D) submitted willingly to fate, even though her submission caused her death.

(E) did not set the tragic process in motion, but is still a tragic figure.

6. In the author's opinion, an act of humility in comedy is most analogous to

(A) a catastrophe in tragedy.

(B) an ironic action in tragedy.

(C) a tragic hero's pride and passion

(D) a tragic hero's aversion to sin.

(E) a tragic hero's pursuit of an unusual destiny.

Passage 2

Researchers of women's history point to the early nineteenth century as a time when middle-class women were increasingly isolated in the home, and consequently were considered a group with problems and interests separate from those of men. "The cult of true womanhood" established for such women a special "sphere," and their activities and concerns were supposedly circumscribed by their capabilities for nurturing and teaching. According to the tenets of the cult of true womanhood, the activities within the women's domain made as important a contribution to society as those of men, though different.

Welter has argued that men, not women, were responsible for defining women's social roles. Sklar has challenged Welter's thesis in her work on educator Catharine Beecher. Sklar contends that Beecher, who created many organizational opportunities for women, developed an ideology of womanhood that stressed self-sacrifice and the adoption of active social roles by women in areas such as teaching and moral leadership.

Indeed, in the nineteenth century women's benevolent organizations proliferated. These organizations can be seen as a logical extension of the cult of true womanhood. However, some historians argue that women took this restrictive ideology and cleverly turned it to their own ends. Through these organizations, women found outlets for their talents, developed a positive self-image and a sense of group identity, and learned organizational skills. Moreover, in these groups women gained awareness of the inequalities suffered by women and began to form and participate in women's rights movements.

7. The primary purpose of the passage is to

    (A) trace the roots of the twentieth-century women's rights movement.
    (B) refute the argument of some historians that Catharine Beecher was a supporter of the cult of true womanhood.
    (C) present historians' interpretations of the opportunities open to middle-class women in nineteenth century society.

(D) support Sklar's contention that there were organizational opportunities available to women in the nineteenth century.

(E) report the findings of recent historical research concerning women's organizations in the nineteenth century.

8. Which of the following is most clearly compatible with the principles of the cult of true womanhood as described in the passage?

(A) Women should be encouraged to take an active role in public life.
(B) Women of different social classes do not share the same concerns and interests.
(C) Women should have equal rights with men in both the private and public spheres.
(D) Women should exercise their special talents within a limited setting.
(E) The suitability of an activity for any person should not be decided on the basis of gender.

9. According to the passage, Sklar's study of Catharine Beecher showed that

(A) nineteenth century women contributed to the defining of women's roles in society.
(B) the life-styles available limited their ability to use their talents.
(C) women's roles in the nineteenth century were expanding more rapidly than ever before.
(D) the cult of true womanhood was not as influential in the nineteenth century as scholars had previously thought.
(E) few nineteenth century women were as influential as Beecher was in promoting women's rights.

10. In the second paragraph, the approach of the author to the discussion of historians' views regarding the roles of nineteenth-century women can best be described as that of

(A) an enthusiastic advocate of women's rights.
(B) an objective reporter of historical theories.
(C) a dispassionate historical theorist.
(D) a biased compiler of historical facts.
(E) a doctrinaire interpreter of women's history.

11. All of the following are mentioned in the passage as advantages of participation in a nineteenth century women' organization EXCEPT

(A) enjoyment of public admiration.

(B) attainment of increased self-confidence.

(C) effective use of capabilities.

(D) acquisition of new skills.

(E) development of a sense of unity with other women.

12. The passage suggests that subscribers to the ideals of the cult of true womanhood saw women as

(A) rivals of men.

(B) unproductive partners of men.

(C) influential social reformers.

(D) willing players of roles complementary to those of men.

(E) dedicated feminists committed to equal rights for women.

Passage 3

Poetic justice in medieval and Elizabethan literature seems so satisfying that twentieth-century scholars are determined to find further examples. In fact, these scholars have merely forced victimized characters into a moral framework by which the injustices inflicted on them are, somehow or other, justified.

Writers often encouraged their readers to side with their tragic heroines by describing injustices so cruel that readers cannot help but join in protest. By portraying Griselda in The Clerk's Tale, as a meek, gentle victim who does not criticize or rebel against the persecutor, her husband Walter, Chaucer incites readers to espouse Griselda's cause. Similarly, to assert that Webster's Duchess deserved torture and death because she chose to marry the man she loved and to bear their children is, in effect, to join forces with her tyrannical brothers and thus confound the operation of poetic justice, with precisely those examples of social injustice that Webster does everything in his power to make readers condemn.

Thus Chaucer and Webster attack injustice, argue on behalf of the victims and prosecute the persecutors. Their readers serve as a court of appeal that remains free to rule, as the evidence requires, in favor of the innocent and injured parties. To paraphrase Samuel Johnson: Despite all the dogmatism of learning, it is by the common sense and compassion of readers who are uncorrupted by the prejudices of some opinionated school that the characters and situations in medieval and Elizabethan literature can best be judged.

13. The primary purpose of the passage is to

   (A) describe the role of the tragic heroine in medieval and Elizabethan literature.
   (B) resolve a controversy over the meaning of "poetic justice" as it is discussed in certain medieval and Elizabethan literary treatises.
   (C) present evidence to support the view that characters in medieval and Elizabethan tragedies are to blame for their fates.
   (D) assert that it is impossible for twentieth-century readers to fully comprehend the characters and situations in medieval and Elizabethan literary works.
   (E) argue that some twentieth-century scholars have misapplied the concept of "poetic justice" in analyzing certain medieval and Elizabethan literary works.

14. It can be inferred from the passage that the author considers Chaucer's Griselda to be

   (A) an innocent victim.
   (B) an imprudent person.
   (C) a rebellious daughter.
   (D) a strong individual
   (E) an overbearing wife

15. It can be inferred from the passage that the author believes that most people respond to intended instances of poetic justice in medieval and Elizabethan literature with

   (A) annoyance
   (B) disapproval
   (C) indifference
   (D) amusement
   (E) gratification

16. As described in the passage, the process by which some twentieth-century scholars have reached their conclusions about the blameworthiness of victims in medieval and Elizabethan literary works is most similar to which of the following?

   (A) Derivation of logically sound conclusions from well-founded premises.
   (B) Accurate observation of data, inaccurate calculation of statistics and drawing incorrect conclusions from the faulty statistics.
   (C) Establishment of a theory, application of the theory to ill-fitting data, and drawing unwarranted conclusions from the data.
   (D) Development of two schools of thought about a factual situation, debate between the two schools and rendering of a balanced judgment by an objective observer.
   (E) Consideration of a factual situation by a group, discussion of various possible explanatory hypotheses, and agreement by consensus on the most plausible explanation.

Passage 4

Archaeology as a profession faces two major problems. First, only paltry sums are available for excavating and even less is available for publishing the results and preserving excavated sites. Second, there is the problem of illegal excavation, resulting in museum-quality pieces being sold to the highest bidder.

I would like to make an outrageous suggestion that would both provide funds for archaeology and reduce the amount of illegal digging: Sell excavated artifacts on the open market. Such sales would provide substantial funds for excavation and preservation and simultaneously break the illegal excavator's grip on the market. You might object that professionals excavate to acquire knowledge, not money. Moreover, ancient artifacts are part of our global cultural heritage, which should be available for all to appreciate, not sold to the highest bidder. I agree. Sell nothing that has unique artistic merit or scientific value. But, you might reply, every artifact has scientific value. Here we part company.

I refer to the thousands of artifacts that are essentially duplicates of one another. In one excavation in Cyprus, archaeologists found 2,000 virtually indistinguishable small jugs in a single courtyard. The basements of museums are simply not large enough to store the artifacts that are likely to be discovered in the future. There is not enough money even to catalogue the finds; as a result, they cannot be found again and become as inaccessible as if they had never been discovered. With computerized cataloging prior to sale, sold artifacts could be more accessible than are the pieces stored in crowded museum basements.

17. The primary purpose of the passage is to propose

   (A) an alternative to museum display of artifacts
   (B) a way to curb illegal digging while benefiting the archaeological profession
   (C) a way to distinguish artifacts with scientific value from those that have no such value
   (D) the governmental regulation of archaeological sites
   (E) a new system for cataloguing duplicate artifacts

18. The author implies that all of the following statements about duplicate artifacts are true EXCEPT:

(A) A market for such artifacts already exists.

(B) Such artifacts seldom have scientific value.

(C) There is likely to be a continuing supply of such artifacts.

(D) Museums are well supplied with examples of such artifacts.

(E) Such artifacts frequently exceed in quality those already catalogued in museum collections.

19. Which of the following is mentioned in the passage as a disadvantage of storing artifacts in museum basements?

(A) Museum officials rarely allow scholars access to such artifacts.

(B) Space that could be better used for display is taken up for storage.

(C) Artifacts discovered in one excavation often become separated from each other.

(D) Such artifacts are often damaged by variations in temperature and humidity.

(E) Such artifacts often remain uncatalogued and thus cannot be located once they are put in storage.

20. The author mentions the excavation in Cyprus to emphasize which of the following points?

(A) Ancient lamps and pottery vessels are less valuable, although more rare, than royal seal impressions.

(B) Artifacts that are very similar to each other present cataloguing difficulties to archaeologists.

(C) Artifacts that are not uniquely valuable, and therefore could be sold, are available in large quantities.

(D) Cyprus is the most important location for unearthing large quantities of salable artifacts.

(E) Illegal sales of duplicate artifacts are wide-spread, particularly on the island of Cyprus.

21. Which pair of terms best describes the tone of the passage?

(A) satirical and rancorous

(B) emotional and ambiguous

(C) neutral and descriptive

(D) reasoned but opinionated

(E) critical and satirical

22. The author anticipates which of the following initial objections to the adoption of his proposal?

(A) Museum officials will become unwilling to store artifacts.

(B) An oversupply of salable artifacts will result and the demand for them will fall.

(C) Artifacts that would have been displayed in public places will be sold to private collectors.

(D) Illegal excavators will have an even larger supply of artifacts for resale.

(E) Counterfeiting of artifacts will become more commonplace.

Passage 5

Most successful senior managers do not closely follow the classical rational model of first clarifying goals, assessing the problem, formulating options, estimating likelihoods of success, making a decision, and only then taking action. Rather, these senior executives rely on what is vaguely termed "intuition" to manage a network of interrelated problems that require them to deal with ambiguity, inconsistency, novelty, and surprise.

Isenberg's recent research on the cognitive processes of senior managers reveals that they use intuition in at least five distinct ways. First, they intuitively sense when a problem exists. Second, managers rely on intuition to perform well-learned behavior patterns rapidly. A third function of intuition is to synthesize isolated bits of data and practice into an integrated picture, often in an "Aha!" experience. Fourth, some managers use intuition as a check on the results of more rational analysis. Finally, managers can use intuition to bypass in-depth analysis and move rapidly to engender a plausible solution. Used in this way, intuition is an almost instantaneous cognitive process in which a manager recognizes familiar patterns.

One of the implications of the intuitive style of executive management is that "thinking" is inseparable from acting. Since managers often "know" what is right before they can analyze and explain it, they frequently act first and explain later. Analysis is inextricably tied to action in thinking/acting cycles, in which managers develop thoughts about their companies and organizations not by analyzing a problematic situation and then acting, but by acting and analyzing in close concert.

23. According to the passage, senior managers use intuition in all of the following ways EXCEPT to

(A) speed up of the creation of a solution to a problem
(B) identify a problem
(C) ring together disparate facts
(D) stipulate clear goals
(E) evaluate possible solutions to a problem

24. Which of the following terms best describes the tone of the passage?

   (A) critical.
   (B) biased.
   (C) emotional.
   (D) subjective.
   (E) analytical.

25. Which of the following best exemplifies "an 'Aha!' experience" as it is presented in the passage?

   (A) A manager risks taking an action whose outcome is unpredictable to discover whether the action changes the problem at hand.
   (B) A manager performs well-learned and familiar behavior patterns in creative and uncharacteristic ways to solve a problem.
   (C) A manager suddenly connects seemingly unrelated facts and experiences to create a pattern relevant to the problem at hand.
   (D) A manager rapidly identifies the methodology used to compile data yielded by systematic analysis.
   (E) A manager swiftly decides which of several sets of tactics to implement in order to deal with the contingencies suggested by a problem.

26. According to the passage, the classical model of decision analysis includes all of the following EXCEPT

   (A) evaluation of a problem
   (B) creation of possible solutions to a problem
   (C) establishment of clear goals to be reached by the decision
   (D) action undertaken in order to discover more information about a problem
   (E) comparison of the probable effects of different solutions to a problem

27. It can be inferred from the passage that which of the following would most probably be one major difference in behavior between Manager X, who uses intuition to reach decisions, and Manager Y, who uses only formal decision analysis?

    (A) Manager X analyzes first and then acts; Manager Y does not.
    (B) Manager X checks possible solutions to a problem by systematic analysis; Manager Y does not
    (C) Manager X takes action in order to arrive at the solution to a problem; Manager Y does not.
    (D) Manager Y draws on years of hands-on experience in creating a solution to a problem; Manager X does not.
    (E) Manager Y depends on day-to-day tactical maneuvering; Manager X does not.

28. The passage provides support for which of the following statements?

    (A) Managers who rely on intuition are more successful than those who rely on formal decision analysis.
    (B) Managers cannot justify their intuitive decisions.
    (C) Managers' intuition works contrary to their rational and analytical skills
    (D) Logical analysis of a problem increases the number of possible solutions.
    (E) Intuition enables managers to employ their practical experience more efficiently.

Passage Set 1: Answers with Explanations

1. The passage juxtaposes two contradictory theories of tragedy. See the first sentence of para 1. Hence, (A).

2. No tenable middle ground can be sought when two disparate theories are juxtaposed. Refer to para 1. Hence, (D).

3. Finding tone to be "objective" (C, the correct answer here) usually requires eliminating other tones that would be subjective. Although the passage expresses dissatisfaction with both theories, it considers both of them, so it cannot be called dismissive. An ironic tone would require some clue that the author means something different than what he or she is literally saying, and there are no clues of that kind in the passage. The author does not use any highly emotional language that would suggest anger or worry. Hence, (C).

4. From the third sentence of the second paragraph to the end of the paragraph, the theory presented at the beginning of that paragraph is being disproved. Hence, (C). Other answers use phrases directly taken from the passage, which makes them tempting even though they are incorrect. In questions of this type, the relationship between two ideas is critical to finding the right answer.

5. Cordelia is presented as an innocent victim of fate. Hence, (E).

6. Refer to paragraph 2. The author states that "hubris precipitates catastrophe <u>just as</u> in comedy the cause of the happy ending is usually some act of humility." The question asks about an analogy, and the phrase "just as" separates the two parts of the analogy in the sentence. In logical terms, the analogy is "hubris : catastrophe in tragedy :: act of humility : happy ending in comedy." Hence, (C).

7. See the first sentence, which is the topic sentence of the passage. Hence, (C).

8. See the second sentence of para 1: "...their activities and concerns were supposedly circumscribed by their capabilities for nurturing and teaching." Hence, (D).

9. See the last sentence of para 2. Hence, (A).

10. The author does not subjectively critique the findings. Hence, (B).

11. Refer to "women found outlets for their talents, developed a positive self-image and sense of group identity and learned organizational skills" in the last paragraph. No mention is made of enjoyment of public admiration. Hence, (A).

12. See the last sentence of paragraph 1. Hence, (D).

13. The second paragraph undercuts the argument laid out in the first paragraph. In the second paragraph, the author tries to explain this through examples. Again, read the last few lines of the passage: "it is by the common sense and compassion of readers who are uncorrupted by the prejudices of some opinionated school." (E) states a similar argument. Hence, (E).

14. See "Chaucer incites readers to espouse Griselda's cause" in relation to "By portraying Griselda...as a meek, gentle victim who does not criticize, much less rebel against...Walter." Thus, for the author, Griselda is definitely an innocent victim. Hence, (A).

15. Most of the people would respond to poetic justice with gratification because their sense of outrage is vindicated and appeased. Hence, (E).

16. (C) is the appropriate option. The first paragraph discusses an established theory (the theory of poetic justice that occurs in medieval and Elizabethan literature). The second paragraph applies this theory to some examples like that of Griselda and Webster's Duchess, simply to prove it wrong. Concentrate on the latter part of the concluding paragraph. The author tries to refute the theory and comes to a conclusion that the common sense and compassion of readers will judge Medieval and Elizabethan literature correctly, different from the opinionated scholars. Hence, (C).

17. (B) is the best answer. The first paragraph identifies two major problems faced by the archaeological profession: inadequate funding and illegal digging. The author proceeds to propose allowing the sale of excavated artifacts and to explain how this would solve both problems. The author then supports the proposal by countering possible objections to it, and in the last paragraph explains how the proposal would curb illegal digging. Thus, the way information is organized in the passage indicates that the author's purpose is to suggest that allowing the sale of excavated artifacts would provide funds for the archaeological profession and curb illegal digging.

18. (E) is the best answer. The question requires you to identify the answer choice that CANNOT be inferred from the passage. Nothing in the passage implies that duplicate artifacts exceed museum objects in quality.

19. (E) is the best answer. The disadvantages of storing artifacts in museum basements are discussed in the last paragraph. The passage states that "There is not enough money to catalogue the finds" and declares that as a result stored objects cannot be located.

20. (C) is the best answer. The author refutes the assertion that every object excavated has potential scientific value and therefore should not be sold. The author also defines those objects that do not have scientific value: "the thousands of artifacts that essentially duplicate one another." The Cyprus excavation appears in the next sentence as an example of one location in which such duplicate artifacts have been found in large quantities. The reference to "2,000 virtually indistinguishable small jugs" highlights the profusion and uniformity of the Cyprus finds. Thus, the excavation is mentioned in order to emphasize the ready availability of objects that lack unique value and therefore could be sold.

21. We know the passage is opinionated from the signaling phrase "I would like to make an outrageous suggestion." Because the rest of the passage supports this—with reasoned evidence—the best answer is (D). To add speed to your answering of a question like this, use the process of elimination, and remember that if you can eliminate one word from a pair, then you have eliminated the whole answer. For example, if you know that the

passage is not satirical, you don't even need to ask whether or not it is rancorous; you can eliminate (A).

22. (C) is the best answer. The author begins the third sentence of the second paragraph by saying "you might object" in order to anticipate possible objections to the adoption of his proposal. In the next sentence the author asserts that "ancient artifacts should be available for all to appreciate, not sold to the highest bidder," acknowledging an opponent's fear that individuals might be allowed to purchase objects that ought to be displayed in public institutions. This objection is paraphrased in this choice.

23. (D) is the best answer. The question requires you to recognize which of the choices is NOT mentioned in the passage as a way in which senior managers use intuition. The passage does not mention stipulating goals.

24. The passage describes a general topic in the first paragraph, reports on research about the specifics of that topic in the second paragraph, and explains an implication of that research in the third paragraph. This is a classic analysis, so the best answer is (E). If you're not sure, use the process of elimination. The passage has no particular subject of criticism, eliminating (A); no discernible bias, eliminating (B); does not demonstrate an identifiable emotional attitude toward its material, eliminating (C); and does not express personal opinion, eliminating (D).

25. (C) is the best answer. An "Aha! Experience" is said to result from the synthesizing of "isolated bits of data and practice into an integrated picture." This choice is the best example of this kind of process. The connecting of seemingly unrelated facts and experiences mentioned in the answer choice is equivalent to synthesizing "isolated bits of data and practice," and the pattern referred to is comparable to an "integrated picture."

26. (D) is the best answer. The question requires you to recognize which of the choices is NOT mentioned in the passage as a component of the classical model of decision

analysis. Only this choice, "action undertaken in order to discover more information about a problem," does not appear in the passage.

27. (C) is the best answer. The question requires you to compare behavior based on intuition with behavior based on formal decision analysis. This choice specifies that the manager who uses intuition incorporates action into the decision-making process, but the manager who uses formal analysis does not. This distinction is made in several places in the passage. The first paragraph emphasizes that decision-making and action-taking are separate steps in formal decision analysis: "making a decision, and only then taking action." On the other hand, those who use intuition "integrate action into the process of thinking." Again, the author mentions that in the intuitive style of management, "thinking is inseparable from acting," and "analysis is inextricably tied to action."

28. (E) is the best answer. The question requires you to identify a statement that can be inferred from information in the passage but is not explicitly stated. The author asserts that intuitive managers can "move rapidly to engender a plausible solution" and that their intuition is based on "well-learned behavior patterns." This implies that the combination of skill and rapidity enables managers to employ their practical experience more efficiently, as this choice states.

PASSAGE SET 2

This passage set consists of above-average difficulty passages and questions.

PASSAGE 1

From ancient times, men have believed that life could arise spontaneously: from the ooze of rivers could come eels, worms from mud, maggots from dead meat. The centuries gradually disintegrated men's belief in the spontaneous origin of maggots, but the doctrine of generation clung tenaciously to the question of bacterial origin.

John Needham declared that he could bring about at will the creation of living microbes in heat-sterilized broths. Abbe Spallanzani responded with an experiment showing that a broth sealed from the air while boiling never develops bacterial growths. Into the controversy came Louis Pasteur, who believed that solving this problem was essential to developing his theories about bacteria in nature. Pasteur acknowledged that living bacteria might arise from inanimate matter. To him the research task was to repeat the work of those who claimed to have observed bacterial entry. Pasteur worked logically. He found that after prolonged boiling, a broth would ferment only when air was admitted to it. Therefore, he contended that either air contained a factor necessary for spontaneous generation of life or viable germs were borne in by the air and seeded in the sterile broth. Using flasks designed to exclude air, Pasteur found that when their necks were snapped to admit air, bacterial growth would commence - but an occasional flask would remain sterile. Trying to control the ingredients, he used water from clear wells that had been rendered germ free by slow filtration through sandy soil. This discovery led to the familiar porcelain filters of the bacteriology lab.

The argument went beyond science and became a burning religious and philosophical question. For many, Pasteur's conclusions caused conflict because they seemed simultaneously to support the Biblical account of creation while denying other philosophical systems. The public was subjected to lectures and debates between exponents of both views. Perhaps the most famous of these was Pasteur's 1864 lecture at the Sorbonne in which he showed his audience the swan necked flasks containing sterile broths and concluded, "I have taken my drop of water from the immensity of creation, and I have taken it full of the elements appropriated to the development of inferior beings, and I wait, I watch, I question it! ... But it is dumb, since these experiments begun several years ago; it is dumb because I kept it from the only thing man does not know how to produce: from the germs that float in the air, from life, for life is a germ and germ is life. Never will the doctrine of spontaneous generation recover from the mortal blow of this simple experiment." Despite the ringing declaration of Pasteur, the issue did not die completely. And although far from healthy, it is not yet dead.

I believe spontaneous generation is not only possible but completely reasonable. Science has rationally concluded that life originated on earth by spontaneous generation. In the controversy between Pasteur and spontaneous generationists, what was unreasonable was the parade of men who claimed to have proved spontaneous generation in the face of proof that their work was full of errors.

1. As portrayed in the passage, which statement below best describes the relationship between Needham and Spallanzani's theories?
    (A) Needham essentially agreed with Spallanzani but added detail to Spallanzani's theory.
    (B) Spallanzani's theory supported Needham's theory.
    (C) Spallanzani attempted to refute Needham.
    (D) Needham discredited Spallanzani by attacking his lack of religion.
    (E) Spallanzani responded to Needham with an experiment that proved the possibility of spontaneous generation.

2. The tone of this passage shifts in the final paragraph because:
    (A)   The author suddenly reverses his argument.
    (B)   It is the first introduction of personal opinion.
    (C)   The author reveals that he believes spontaneous generation is unreasonable.
    (D)   The first paragraph is highly emotional and the last paragraph is not.
    (E)   A different author clearly wrote the final paragraph.

3. According to the passage:

    (A) Pasteur's precursors in the field worked on the basis of spontaneous generation.
    (B) Unlike his predecessors Pasteur worked on logical premises rather than arbitrary and spontaneous discoveries.
    (C) Pasteur stood to benefit largely from the work of his predecessors.
    (D) Pasteur developed the idea set forth by Voltaire and Needham.
    (E) Pasteur laid the issue to rest conclusively.

4. Pasteur began his work on the basis of the contention that:

    (A) either air contained a factor necessary for the spontaneous generation of life or viable germs were borne in by the air and seeded in the sterile nutrient broth.
    (B) after prolonged boiling, a broth would ferment only when air was admitted to it.
    (C) Pasteur's experiments did not provide evidence against spontaneous generation.
    (D) Neither (a) nor (b)
    (E) Both (a) and (b)

5. The porcelain filters of the bacteriology laboratories owed their descent to:

    (A) Pasteur's homeland
    (B) the well water that had been rendered germ free by slow filtration through sandy soil
    (C) Both (a) and (b)
    (D) experiments in bacteriology
    (E) None of the above

6. What, according to the passage, was Pasteur's declaration to the world?

    (A) Nobody could deny the work done by him
    (B) Science would forever be indebted to his experiments in bacteriology
    (C) The doctrine of spontaneous generation would never recover from the mortal blow dealt to it by his experiments

(D) Those who refused to acknowledge his experiments would regret their skepticism

(E) The doctrine of spontaneous generation was proved conclusively wrong.

7. What according to the author, was the problem with the proponents of spontaneous generation?

(A) Their work had no scientific basis

(B) Their work was ruined by experimental errors

(C) Their work did provided conclusive evidence.

(D) Neither (a) nor (b)

(E) Both (a) and (b)

8. Which statement best describes the author's relationship to the debate described in the passage?

(A) The author believes that spontaneous combustion is possible, although the early researchers had flaws in their experimental methods.

(B) The author views the idea of spontaneous combustion with derision.

(C) The author argues in favor of spontaneous combustion on religious grounds.

(D) The author expresses no opinion about spontaneous combustion.

(E) The author believes spontaneous combustion can only occur in Pasteur's special flasks.

9. One of the reasons for the conflict caused by Pasteur's experiments was that:

(A) they denied the existence of God as the creator

(B) they seemed simultaneously to support the Biblical account of creation while denying a variety of other philosophical systems

(C) academicians and scientists refused to accept his theories

(D) there were too many debates on the topic and this left the people confused

(E) they were inconclusive

10. According to the author:

(A) Spontaneous generation is not possible

(B) Pasteur could not hold his own against the contenders

(C) Science has concluded that life originated by spontaneous generation

(D) Spallanzani showed that spontaneous generation was possible

(E) The idea of spontaneous generation is not reasonable

PASSAGE 2

The highest priced words are ghostwritten by gagmen who furnish the raw material for comedy over the air and on the screen. They have a word-lore all of their own, which they practice for five to fifteen hundred dollar a week, or fifteen dollars a gag at piece rates.

Quite apart from the dollar sign on it, gagmen's word-lore is worth a close look, if you are given to the popular American pastime of playing with words – or if you are part of the 40 percent who make their living in the word trade.

Gag writers' "tricks" with words point up the fact that we have two distinct levels of language: familiar, ordinary words that everybody knows; and elaborate words that don't turn up very often, but many of which we need to know if we are to feel at home in listening to and reading these writers' works.

To be sure, gagmen play with the big words, making not sense but fun of them. They keep on confusing bigotry with bigamy, illiterate with illegitimate, monotony with monogamy, osculation with oscillation. They trade on the fact that for many listeners, these fancy terms linger in a twilight zone of meaning. It's their deliberate intent to make everybody feel cozy at hearing big words, jumbled up or smacked down. After all, such words loom up over-sized in ordinary talk, so no wonder they get the bulldozer treatment from the gagmen.

Their wrecking technique incidentally reveals our language as full of tricky words, some with nineteen different meanings, others which sound alike but differ in sense. For their puns to ring true, gag writers have to know their way around in the language. They don't get paid for ignorance, only for simulating it.

Gagmen's maneuvers are of real concern to anyone who follows words with a fully awakened interest. For the very fact that gag writers often use a long and unusual word as the hinge of a joke or as a peg for situation comedy tells us something quite significant: they are well aware of the limitations of the average vocabulary and are quite willing to cash in on its shortcomings.

When Fred Allen's joke-smiths work out a fishing routine, they have Allen referring to the bait in his most archaic and solemn tones: "I presume you mean the legless invertebrate." This is the old minstrel tick, using a long fancy term, instead of calling a worm a worm.

And even the high-brow radio writers have taken advantage of gagmen's technique you might never expect to hear on the air such words as lepidopterist and entomologist. Both occur in a very famous radio play by Norman Corvine, "My client Curly," about an unusual caterpillar that would dance to the tune "Yes, sir, she's my baby" but remained inert to all other music. The dancing caterpillar was given a real New York buildup, which involved calling in the experts on butterflies and insects that travel under the learned names above. Corvine made mild fun of the fancy professional titles, at the same time explaining them unobtrusively.

There are many similar occasions where any one working with words can turn gagmen's trade secrets to cash. Just what words do they think are outside the familiar range? How do they pick the words that they "kick around?" It is not hard to find out.

11. According to the writer, a large part of the American population:

   (A) indulges in playing out the role of gag writers
   (B) indulges in the word trade
   (C) seeks employment in the gag trade
   (D) looks down on gag writers
   (E) admires gag writers

12. The hallmark of gag writers is that they:

   (A) ruin good, simple language
   (B) have fun with words
   (C) make better sense of words
   (D) play with words to suit the audience's requirements
   (E) need not be good with the language

13. According to the passage, the second level of language is important if:

    (A) one wants to feel at home reading and listening today
    (B) one wants to be a gag writer
    (C) one wants to understand clean entertainment
    (D) one wants to be successful
    (E) None of the above

14. According to the writer, gag writers thrive on:

    (A) the double-layered aspect of language
    (B) using long and unusual words
    (C) vulgar innuendoes
    (D) commonplace jugglery with language
    (E) the audience's inability to understand double meaning

15. In the gag writers' trade:

    (A) long words are abbreviated for effect
    (B) parts of words are combined to produce completely new words
    (C) long words play a major role
    (D) Both (b) and (c)
    (E) None of above

16. When the writer says, "They don't get paid for ignorance, only for simulating it," he
    means to say:

    (A) the audience likes to think the gag writers are an ignorant lot
    (B) gag writers are terrific with insinuations
    (C) simulating ignorance is the trick that makes gag writers tick
    (D) None of the above
    (E) All of the above

17. Gag writers have influenced:

   (A) television artists
   (B) radio writers
   (C) circus clowns
   (D) television hosts
   (E) actors

PASSAGE 3

If western civilization is in a state of permanent crisis, perhaps something is wrong with its education. No civilization has ever devoted more energy and resources to education; we believe that education is the key to everything. Whatever the problem, the answer must be more and better education.

Lord Snow, in his *Rede Lecture*, expressed his concern that "the intellectual life of the whole of western civilization is increasingly being split into two polar groups...At one pole we have the literary intellectuals...at the other scientists." He deplores the "gulf of mutual incomprehension" between these groups and wants it bridged. His educational plan would be, first, to get as many "alpha-plus scientists" as possible; second, to train a larger stratum of professionals to do the supporting research, design, and development; third, to train thousands of other scientists and engineers; and fourth to train politicians, administrators and entire communities who know enough science to understand the concepts. Thus, Lord Snow suggests, the "Two Cultures" may communicate. These ideas leave one with the uncomfortable feeling that ordinary people are of little use; they have failed to make the grade but should be educated enough to know what the scientists mean when they talk.

If we rely so much on the power of education to enable ordinary people to cope with the problems generated by science and technology, then there must be something more to education than Lord Snow suggests. Science and engineering know-how is no more a culture than a piano is music. Can education help us to turn the potentiality into a reality?

To do so the task of education would be first and foremost the transmission of ideas of value. We must also transmit know-how but this must take second place; it is foolhardy to give people great powers without ensuring that they have a reasonable idea of what to do with them. Today mankind is in mortal danger, not because we are short of scientific know-how, but because we use it without wisdom. The essence of education is the transmission of values, but values do not help us to pick our way through life unless we assimilate and use them. When we begin to think we can do so only because our mind is already filled with ideas. We often notice the existence of fixed ideas in other people's minds, ideas with which they think without being aware of doing so. We call them prejudices, but the word prejudice is generally applied to ideas that are erroneous. Most ideas with which we think are not of that kind. Some ideas, like those found in words and grammar, cannot be described in terms of truth or error. Others are not prejudices, but the result of judgment.

I say, therefore, that we think with ideas and that what we call thinking is the application of pre-existing ideas to a given situation. The way we think depends on the kinds of ideas that fill our minds. If these ideas are small and weak, it is difficult to bear the resultant feeling of emptiness, and the vacuum may only too easily be filled by some big notion that suddenly seems to give meaning and purpose to our existence. We feel that education will help solve each new problem or complexity that arises. Herein lies one of the great dangers of our times. When people ask for education they normally mean something more than mere training, more than knowledge of facts, more than a diversion. I think what they are really looking for are ideas that could make the world, and their own lives, intelligible to them.

18. The writer's contention in the passage is that the crisis in Western civilization can be explained by:

   (A) the presence of some flaws in its education
   (B) some inherent lack of coordination among its various elements
   (C) some basic misunderstanding in its society
   (D) the energy it has devoted to education
   (E) the conflict between scientists and literary intellectuals

19. According to the writer, Lord Snow sees the intellectual life of western society as split between:

   (A) the educated and the uneducated
   (B) the government servants and the plebeians
   (C) scientists and literary intellectuals
   (D) administrators and intellectuals
   (E) philosophers and administrators

20. Which of the following best describes the tone of the passage?

    (A) analytical and objective
    (B) analytical and opinionated
    (C) analytical and emotional
    (D) ambiguous and descriptive
    (E) ambiguous and emotional

21. What according to the author, would be the definition of prejudice?

    (A) Ideas that help people to identify with new situations
    (B) Fixed ideas that are often erroneous
    (C) Ideas that people cull from experience in order to judge a situation
    (D) Fixed ideas that see a person through the trials and tribulations of life
    (E) None of the above

22. According to Lord Snow, which of the following groups needs to be educated enough
    to at least understand the works of scientists and engineers?

    (A) Politicians, administrators, entire communities
    (B) Politicians and literary intellectuals
    (C) Politician and the laymen
    (D) Politicians and philosophers
    (E) Only politicians

23. In the passage, the writer questions:

    (A) the neutrality of science
    (B) scientists' stands on the neutrality of science
    (C) Lord Snow's assertions on education
    (D) the value of education
    (E) the role of prejudice in education

24. The author's assertion in the passage is that education's main responsibility is to:

(A) transmit values

(B) transmit technical knowledge

(C) both (a) and (b)

(D) transmit ideas regarding human and societal norms

(E) cause harmonious relationships between different groups

25. The author believes that:

(A) the gulf between science and literature needs to be bridged

(B) ideas should be maintained for a holistic view of society and its problems

(C) words are not ideas

(D) none of the above

(E) all of the above

26. Which of the following sentences is not true according to the author?

(A) values can help us pick our way through life

(B) values are merely dogmatic assertions

(C) one identifies with values

(D) ideas of value are needed to make the world intelligible

(E) the essence of education is transmission of values

27. According to the author, "Thinking" is:

(A) being

(B) knowing

(C) application of pre-existing ideas to a situation

(D) application of fixed ideas to a situation

(E) the essence of living

PASSAGE 4

The persistent patterns in the way nations fight reflect their traditions and deeply rooted attitudes that collectively make up their unique cultures. In the Vietnam War, the strategic tradition of the US called for forcing the enemy to fight a massed battle, where superior American weapons would prevail. The US was trying to re-fight World War II, against an enemy with no intention of doing the same.

The Asian way of war is indirect, avoiding frontal attacks meant to overpower an opponent. This springs from Asian history and geography: the great distances and harsh terrain often made it difficult to execute the sort of open field clashes allowed by the flat terrain and compact size of Europe. In Sun-tzu's The Art of War and other Chinese writings, the highest achievement of arms is to defeat an adversary without fighting. War contains too many surprises to be a first resort. It can lead to ruinous losses and inspire heroic efforts in an enemy, as the US learned in Vietnam.

Aware of the uncertainties of a military campaign, Sun-tzu advocated war only after the most thorough preparations. Even then it should be quick and clean. Ideally, the army only deals the final blow to an enemy already weakened by isolation, poor morale, and disunity. Ever since Sun-tzu, the Chinese have been seen as masters of subtlety who take measured actions to manipulate an adversary without his knowledge. The dividing line between war and peace can be obscure. Low level violence often is the backdrop to a larger strategic campaign. The victim, focused on the day-to-day events, never realizes what's happening until it's too late. The Viet Cong lured French and US infantry deep into the jungle, weakening their morale over several years. The mobile army of the US was designed to fight on the plains of Europe, where it could quickly move unhindered from one spot to the next. The jungle did more than make quick movement impossible; broken down into smaller units and scattered in isolated bases, U.S. forces were deprived of the feeling of support and protection that ordinarily comes from being part of a big army. By altering the way the war was fought, the Viet Cong stripped the US of its belief in inevitable victory.

The greatest military surprises in US history have all been in Asia. Pearl Harbor, the Chinese intervention in Korea, and the Tet offensive all came out of a tradition of stealth. US intelligence in determining the location and movements of enemy units improved after each surprise, but no improvement in their ability to foresee what would happen next was in evidence. This is a cultural, as well as a technical, divide.

The West's great strategic writer, Clausewitz, linked war to politics, as did Sun-tzu. Both opposed militarism. There all similarity ends. Clausewitz wrote that the way to achieve a political purpose is to destroy the enemy's army. Morale and unity are important, but they should be harnessed in the ultimate battle. If the Eastern way of war is embodied by the stealthy archer, the metaphorical Western counterpart is the swordsman charging forward, seeking a decisive showdown. Sun-tzu's great disciple Ho Chi Minh is respected in Asia for his use of intellect and deception to attain advantage over a stronger adversary. But in the West, his approach is seen as underhanded and *devious*. To the American strategic mind, the Viet Cong did not fight fairly. They should have come out into the open and fought like men, instead of hiding in the jungle, sneaking around.

28. According to the author, the main reason for the U.S. losing the Vietnam war was:

    (A) the Vietnamese understood the local terrain better
    (B) the lack of support for the war from the American people
    (C) the failure of the US to mobilize its military strength
    (D) their inability to fight a war on terms other than those they understood well
    (E) they wanted to fight in the open like men

29. Which of the following statements does not describe the "Asian" way of war?

    (A) indirect attacks without frontal attacks
    (B) the swordsman charging forward to obliterate the enemy once and for all
    (C) Manipulation of all adversaries without their knowledge
    (D) subduing an enemy without fighting
    (E) winning the war without direct fighting

30. Which of the following is not one of Sun-tzu's ideas?

   (A) actual combat is the principal means of subduing an adversary
   (B) war should be undertaken only after through preparation
   (C) war is linked to politics
   (D) war should not be left to the generals alone
   (E) wars can prove costly in terms of men and material

31. The difference in the concepts of war of Clausewitz and Sun-tzu is best characterized
   by:

   (A) Clausewitz's support for militarism as against Sun-tzu's opposition to it
   (B) their linking of war with politics
   (C) their attitude to guerilla warfare
   (D) their different about using stealth in war
   (E) none of the above

32. To the Americans, the approach of the Viet Cong seemed devious because:

   (A) the Viet Cong did not fight like men out in the open
   (B) the Viet Cong allied with America's enemies
   (C) the Viet Cong took strategic advice from Mao Zedong
   (D) the Viet Cong used bows and arrows rather than conventional weapons
   (E) the Viet Cong did not indulge in guerilla warfare

33. According to the author, the greatest military surprises in American history have been
   in Asia because:

   (A) the Americans failed to implement their military strategies many miles away from
       their own country
   (B) the Americans were unable to use their technologies like intelligence satellites
       effectively to detect enemy movements

(C) the Americans failed to understand the Asian culture of war that was based on stealth and surprise

(D) Clausewitz is inferior to Sun-tzu

(E) Asia is too far away for America to fight

PASSAGE 5

Since World War II, the nation–state has been endorsed by every political system. In the name of modernization in the West, of socialism in the Eastern Block, and of development in the Third World, it was expected to guarantee the happiness of individuals and of societies. However, the state today appears to have broken down. It has failed to guarantee security or social justice, and has been unable to prevent international or civil wars. Distributed by the claims of communities within it, the nation-state tries to repress their demands and to proclaim itself as the only guarantor of security of all. In the name of national unity, territorial integrity, equality of all citizens, and nonpartisanship, the state can use its resources to reject the demands of communities; it may even use genocide to ensure order.

In reaction to globalization, individuals and communities everywhere are voicing their desire to exist and to play an active part in national and international life. The current upsurge in demand for the recognition of identities can be looked at in two ways. On the positive side, the assertions of identity by certain groups can be regarded as "liberation movements," challenging oppression and injustice. Their activities – proclaiming that they are different, rediscovering their cultural roots or strengthening group solidarity - may accordingly be seen as legitimate attempts to escape subjugation. On the downside, however, militant action for recognition tends to make such groups more deeply entrenched in their attitudes and to make their cultural compartments even more watertight. The assertion of identity then starts turning into isolation, and is liable to slide into intolerance and towards xenophobia and violence.

Group identity involves simplification, choosing of a limited number of criteria such as religion, language, skin color, and place of origin so that their members recognize themselves in terms of the labels attached to the group. Paradoxically, precisely because identity represents a simplifying fiction, creating uniform groups out of disparate people, that identity performs a cognitive function. It enables us to put names to ourselves and others, form some idea of who we are and who others are, and ascertain the place we occupy along with the others in the world and society. People would not go along as they do, often in large numbers, with the propositions put to them if there was not a very strong feeling of need for identity, a need to know who we are, where we come from, and where we are going.

Identity is thus a necessity in a constantly changing world, but it can also be a potent source of violence and disruption. How can these two contradictory aspects of identity be reconciled? First, we must bear the arbitrary nature of identity categories in mind to remind ourselves that each of us has several identities at the same time. Second, we recognize that culture is constantly being recreated by cobbling together fresh and original elements and counterculture. Finally, the nation–state must respond to the identity urges of its constituent communities and to their legitimate quest for security and social justice. That would guarantee justice both to the state as a whole and its parts, and respect the claims of both reason and emotions. The problem is one of reconciling nationalist demands with exercise of democracy.

34. According to the author, happiness of individuals was expected to be guaranteed in the name of:

   (A) development in the Third World
   (B) socialism in the Third World
   (C) development in the West
   (D) modernization in the Eastern Bloc.
   (E) democracy in the world

35. Demands for recognition of identities can be viewed:

   (A) positively
   (B) as liberation movements and militant action
   (C) as efforts to rediscover cultural roots which can slide towards intolerance of others
   (D) negatively
   (E) all of the above

36. Which of the following best describes the tone of the passage?

   (A) profoundly pessimistic

(B) thoughtlessly optimistic

(C) emotionally clouded

(D) thoughtfully earnest

(E) painfully skeptical

37. According to the author, the nation-state:

(A) has fulfilled its potential

(B) is willing to do anything to preserve order

(C) generates security for all its citizens

(D) has been a major force in preventing civil and international wars

(E) is the best political structure for all its citizens

38. Which of the following views of the nation-state cannot be attributed to the author?

(A) it has not guaranteed peace and security

(B) it may go as far as genocide for self- preservation

(C) it represents the demands of communities within it

(D) it is unable to prevent international wars

(E) it has suppressed subsets of its communities

PASSAGE 6

Man is the means by which things are manifested. It is we who set up a relationship between this tree and that bit of sky. With each of our acts, the world reveals a new face. Though we know that we are directors of being, we also know that we are not its producers. We are inessential in relation to the thing revealed. A chief motive of artistic creation is the need to feel we are essential in relationship to the world. I paint images, having produced them by imposing the unity of mind on the diversity of things. That is, I think myself essential in relation to my creation. But this time it is the created object which escapes me; I cannot reveal and produce at the same time. The creation becomes inessential in relation to the creative activity.

We are less conscious of the thing produced and more conscious of our productive activity. If we ourselves set the rules of production and if our creative drive comes from the heart, then we never find anything but ourselves in our work. Regarding it, we never receive the feeling we put into it. To us, our work never seems objective. When we seek to perceive our work, we recreate it, remembering the operations which produced it. In perception, the object is given as the essential thing and the subject as the inessential. The latter seeks the creation and obtains it, but then the object becomes inessential.

The dialectic is most apparent in writing. To make it concrete reading is necessary. In reading, one foresees the end of the sentence, the next sentence, the next page. He waits for them to confirm or disappoint his foresights. Readers always read in a merely probable future that partly collapses and partly comes together as they progress.

39. The author holds that:

    (A) there is an objective reality and subjective reality
    (B) nature is the sum total of disparate elements
    (C) it is human action that reveals the various facets of nature
    (D) apparently disconnected elements in nature are unified in fundamental sense
    (E) There can be no objectivity in reading

40. It is the author's contention that:

(A) artistic creations are results of human consciousness

(B) the very act of artistic creation leads to the escape of the created object

(C) man can produce and reveal at the same time

(D) an act of creation forces itself on our consciousness leaving us full of amazement

(E) artistic creations are only possible by a certain set of people

41. The passage makes a distinction between perception and creation in terms of:

(A) objectivity and subjectivity

(B) revelation and action

(C) objective reality and perceived reality

(D) essentiality and non-essentiality of objects and subjects

(E) none of the above

42. The art of writing manifests the dialectic of perception and creation because:

(A) the act of reading makes writing concrete

(B) writing, to be meaningful, needs the concrete act of reading

(C) this art is anticipated and progresses on a series of hypotheses

(D) this literary object has a moving horizon brought about by the very act of creation

(E) none of the above

43. A writer as an artist:

(A) reveals the essentiality of revelation

(B) makes us feel essential

(C) creates reality

(D) reveals nature in its permanence

(E) reveals the creativity of nature

PASSAGE 7

Have you ever come across a painting by Picasso, Mondrian, Miro, or any other modern abstract painter, and found yourself engulfed in a brightly colored canvas which your senses cannot interpret? Many people denounce abstractionism as senseless trash. People feel more comfortable with something they can relate to and understand immediately without too much thought. This is the case with the work of Charlie Russell. Being able to recognize the elements in his paintings - trees, horses and cowboys - gives people a safety line to "reality." Some would disagree with my statement that abstract art requires more creativity and artistic talent than does representational art, but there are many weaknesses in their arguments.

People who look down on abstract art have several major arguments to support their beliefs. They feel that artists turn abstract because they are not capable of the technical drafting skills that appear in a Russell. Secondly, they feel that the purpose of art is to create something in an orderly, logical composition. Russell's compositions are balanced and rational: everything sits calmly on the canvas, leaving the viewer satisfied that he has seen all there is to see. The modern abstractionists, on the other hand, seem to compose their pieces irrationally. Finally, many people feel that art should portray the ideal and reality. Russell has been called a great historian because his pieces depict the lifestyle, dress, and events of the times.

I agree in part with many of these arguments, and at one time even endorsed them. But now, I believe differently. Firstly, I object to the argument that abstract artists are not capable of drafting. Many abstract artists, such as Picasso, are excellent draftsmen. As his work matured, Picasso became abstract in order to increase the experiential quality of his work. Guernica was meant as a protest against the bombing of that city by the Germans. To express the terror and suffering of the victims more vividly, he distorted the figures and presented them in a black and white journalistic manner. If he had used representational images and color, much of the emotional content would have been lost and the piece would not have caused the demand for justice that it did. Secondly, I do not think that a piece must be logical and aesthetically pleasing to be art. The message it conveys to its viewers is more important. It should reflect the ideals and issues of its time and be true to itself, not just a flowery, glossy surface. For example, through his work, Mondrian was trying to present a system of simplicity, logic, and rational order. As a result, his piece did end up looking like a scrabble board. Finally, abstract artists and representational artists maintain different ideas about reality. To the abstract artist, reality is what he feels about what his eyes see. This is the reality he interprets on canvas.

The near future may witness the death of representational art through the camera. Within film there is no need to produce detailed historical records manually; the camera does this far more efficiently. Maybe representational art would cease to exist. With abstract art's victory, maybe a different kind of cycle will be touched off. Possibly, thousands of years from now, art itself will be physically non-existent. Some artists today believe that once they have planned a piece mentally, there is no sense in finishing it with their hands; it has already been done and can never be duplicated.

44. The author argues that many people look down upon abstract art because they feel that:

   (A) modern abstract art does not portray what is ideal and real
   (B) abstract artists are unskilled in matters of technical drafting
   (C) abstractionists compose irrationally
   (D) they cannot easily understand it
   (E) all of above

45. The author believes that people feel more comfortable with representational art because:

   (A) it is not engulfed in brightly colored canvases
   (B) they do not have to click their tongues and shake their heads in sympathy
   (C) they understand the art without putting too much strain on their minds
   (D) painting like Guernica do not have a point
   (E) they cannot relate to it easily

46. In the author's opinion, Picasso's Guernica created a strong demand for justice because:

   (A) it was a protest against the German bombing Guernica
   (B) Picasso managed to express the emotional content well with his abstract depiction
   (C) it depicts the terror and suffering of the victims in a distorted manner
   (D) It was a mature work of Picasso's, painted when the artist's drafting skills were excellent
   (E) Picasso was liked by the masses

47. The author acknowledges that Mondrian's pieces may have ended up looking like a scrabble board because:

   (A) Many people declared the poor guy played too many scrabble games
   (B) Mondrian believed in the "grid-work" approach to abstractionist painting
   (C) Mondrian was trying to convey the message of simplicity and rational order.
   (D) Mondrian learned from his Tree series to evolve a grid system
   (E) Mondrian believed in making his work easy to understand

48. The main difference between the abstract artist and the representational artist in the matter of the "ideal" and the "real," according to the author is:

   (A) how each choose to deal with "reality" on his or her canvas
   (B) the inferiority of interpretation of reality over production of reality
   (C) the different values attached by each to being a historian
   (D) the varying levels of drafting skills and logical thinking abilities
   (E) none of the above

PASSAGE 8

The World Trade Organization (WTO) was formed in the early 1990s as a component of the Uruguay Round negotiations. However, it could have been negotiated as part of the Tokyo Round of the 1970s, since that negotiation was an attempt at a "constitutional reform" of the General Agreement on Tariffs and Trade (GATT). Or it could have been put off to the future, as the U.S. Government wanted. What factors led to the creation of the WTO in the early 1990s?

One factor was the pattern of multilateral bargaining that developed late in the Uruguay Round. Like all complex international agreements, the WTO was a product of a series of trade-offs between principal actors and groups. For the United States, which did not want a new organization, the dispute settlement part of the WTO package achieved its longstanding goal of a more effective and more legal dispute settlement system. For the Europeans, who by the 1990s had come to view GATT dispute settlement less in political terms and more as a regime of legal obligations, the WTO package was acceptable as a means to discipline the resort to unilateral measures by the United States. Countries like Canada and other middle and smaller trading partners were attracted by the expansion of a rules-based system and by the symbolic value of a trade organization, both of which inherently support the weak against the strong. The developing countries were attracted due to the provision banning unilateral measures. Finally, and perhaps most important, many countries at the Uruguay Round came to put a higher priority on the export gains than on the import losses that the negotiation would produce, and they came to associate the WTO and rules–based system with those gains. This reasoning - replicated in many countries - was contained in U.S. Ambassador Kantor's defense of the WTO, and it amounted to recognition that international trade and its benefits cannot be enjoyed unless trading nations accept the discipline of a negotiated rules-based environment.

A second factor in the creation of the WTO was pressure from lawyers and the legal process. The dispute settlement system of the WTO was seen as a victory of legalists over pragmatists, but the matter went deeper than that. The GATT and the WTO are contract organizations based on rules, and it is inevitable that an organization created to further rules will in turn be influenced by the legal process. Robert Hudec has written of the "momentum of legal development," but what is this precisely? Legal development can be defined as promotion of the technical legal values of consistency, clarity (or certainty), and effectiveness. These are values that those responsible for administering any legal system will seek to maximize. As it played out in the WTO, consistency meant integrating under one roof the whole lot of separate agreements signed under GATT auspices; clarity meant removing ambiguities about the powers of contracting parties to make certain decisions or to undertake waivers; and effectiveness meant eliminating exceptions arising out of grandfather-rights and resolving defects in dispute settlement procedures and institutional provisions. Concern for these values is inherent in any rules based system of cooperation, since without these values, rules would be meaningless in the first place. Rules, therefore, create their own incentive for fulfillment.

49. What could be the closest reason why the WTO was not formed in the 1970s?

(A) the U.S. Government did not like it
(B) important players did not find it in their best interest to do so
(C) lawyers did not work for the dispute settlement system
(D) the Tokyo Round negotiation was an attempt at constitutional reform
(E) it did not have watertight rules and regulations

50. The most likely reason for the acceptance of the WTO package by nations was that:

(A) it had the means to prevent the U.S. from taking unilateral measure
(B) they recognized the need for a rules-based environment to protect the benefits of increased trade
(C) it settled disputes more legally and more effectively
(D) its rule-based system leads to export gains`
(E) it favored the smaller countries

51. According to the passage, WTO promoted the technical legal values partly through:

(A) integrating under one roof the agreement signed under GATT
(B) propagating rules that create their own incentive for fulfillment

(C) grandfather-rights exceptions and defects in dispute settlement procedures

(D) ambiguities about the powers of contracting parties to make certain decisions

(E) enforcement of European Court regulations

52. Which of the following best describes the tone of the passage?

(A) biased

(B) descriptive

(C) skeptical

(D) analytic

(E) emotional

53. In the statement "...it amounted to a recognition that international trade and its benefits cannot be enjoyed unless trading nations accept the discipline of a negotiated rules-based environment," "it" refers to:

(A) Ambassador Kantor's defense of the WTO

(B) the rules that came out of the GATT agreement

(C) the export gains many countries came to associate with a rules-based system.

(D) the provision of a rules-based system by the WTO

(E) none of the above

54. According to the passage, what are the values encouraged by legal development?

(A) constitutional reform and multilateral bargaining

(B) legal obligations and unilateral measures

(C) rules-based systems and symbolic value

(D) consistency, clarity, and effectiveness

(E) momentum and pragmatism

PASSAGE 9

European pioneers traversed the Alleghenies and began to settle in the Midwest. Beyond the forests, at the western edge of Indiana, they first encountered thousands of miles of the great grass prairie. The wet earth, covered with matted grasses, seemed untillable with their cast iron plows. The pioneers were stymied for nearly two decades until 1837, when blacksmith John Deere invented a steel plow sharp enough to cut through matted grasses and smooth enough to cast off mud. This simple tool opened the prairies to agricultural development.

Sauk County, Wisconsin is the part of the prairie where I have a home. When the Europeans arrived here in 1837, the government forced the native Sauk Indians west of the Mississippi. The settlers used John Deere's invention to open the area for agriculture, ignoring the traditional ways the Sauk had opened the soil for planting. Initially, the land was generous, but each year the soil lost nurturing power. Thirty years later, the land was depleted. Wheat farming became uneconomic; thousands of farmers left Wisconsin seeking fresh land. It took the new European technology just one generation to make this prairie a desert. The Sauk Indians, who knew how to sustain themselves on the prairie, were banished to another kind of desert: a reservation. They forgot the techniques of survival on the prairie. Thus three deserts were created: Wisconsin, the reservation, and the memories of people. Today, this land is populated by the children of a second wave of European farmers. They do not realize that a new settler is coming with an invention as powerful as John Deere's plow.

The new technology, "bereavement counseling," is a tool forged at the state university to "process" grief. Before the new tool's arrival, farmers and townspeople mourn death in the company of neighbors and kin, using lamentation, prayer, and song, heeding the words of the clergy and surrounding themselves in community. Thus they are assured of the bonds between them and renewed in the knowledge that each death matters. Into this prairie community the bereavement counselor arrives with the new technology. The counselor assures the prairie folk of the tool's effectiveness by invoking the name of the university. For some isolated prairie folk, the counselor will approach the County Board and advocate the right to treatment for all. This right will be guaranteed by the Board's decision to reimburse those too poor to pay. Others, schooled to believe in the tools certified by universities, will seek out the counselor by force of habit. Some will use the counselor because the County taxes for the service, so to fail to be counseled is to forego a benefit, even a right. Finally, one day, a Sauk woman's father will die. Her neighbor will not drop by because he doesn't want to interrupt the counselor. Her kin will stay home because they know only the counselor can process grief properly. The clergy will ask the counselor the best form of service to deal with grief. And the grieving daughter will know that only the counselor cares for her because only the counselor comes when death visits. It will be only one generation between when the bereavement counselor arrives and the community of mourners disappears. The counselor's new tool will cut through the social fabric, throwing aside kinship care and neighborly obligations. Like John Deere's plow, the tools of bereavement counseling will create a desert where a community once flourished. Finally, the counselor will see the impossibility of restoring hope in clients once they are genuinely alone. In the failure of the service the bereavement counselor will find the desert in herself.

55. Which one of the following best describes the approach of the author?

(A) comparing experiences with two innovations in order to illustrate the failure of both
(B) presenting community perspective on two technologies which have had negative effects on people
(C) using the negative outcomes of one innovation to illustrate the likely outcomes of another innovation
(D) contrasting two contexts separated in time to illustrate how deserts have arisen
(E) comparing and contrasting two innovations to prove a point.

56. According to the passage, bereavement handling traditionally involves:

(A) the community bereavement counselors working the bereaved to help her overcome grief
(B) the neighbors and kin joining the bereaved and meeting grief together in mourning and prayer

(C) using techniques developed systemically in formal institutions of learning, a trained counselor helping the bereaved cope with grief

(D) the Sauk Indian Chief leading the community with rituals and rites to help lessen the grief of the bereaved

(E) none of the above

57. Due to which of the following reasons, according to the author, will the bereavement counselor find the desert even in herself?

(A) over a period of time working with Sauk Indians who have lost their kinship and relationship she becomes one of them

(B) she is working in an environment where the disappearance of community mourners makes her workplace a social desert

(C) her efforts at grief processing with the bereaved will fail as no amount of professional service can make up for the loss due to the disappearance of community mourners

(D) she has been working with people who have settled for a long time in the Great Desert

(E) she does not personally know the mourners

58. According to the author the bereavement counselor is:

(A) a friend of the bereaved helping him or her handle grief

(B) an advocate of the right treatment for the community

(C) a kin of the bereaved helping him/her handle grief

(D) a formally trained person helping the bereaved handle grief

(E) the only genuine friend of the bereaved

59. The prairie was a great puzzlement for the European pioneers because:

(A) it was covered with thick, untillable layers of grass over a vast stretch

(B) it was a large desert immediately next to lush forests

(C) it was rich cultivable land left fallow for centuries

(D) it could be easily tilled with iron plows

(E) none of the above

60. Which of the following does the desert in the passage refer to?

(A) prairie soil depleted by cultivation wheat

(B) reservation in which native Indians were resettled

(C) absence of and emptiness in community kinship and relationships

(D) all of the above

(E) none of the above

61. According to the author, people will begin to utilize the service of the bereavement counselor because:

(A) new County regulations will make them feel it is a right and if they don't use it, it would be a loss

(B) the bereaved in the community would find her a helpful friend

(C) she will fight for a subsistence allowance from the Country Board for the poor among the bereaved

(D) grief processing needs tools certified by universities and medical centers

(E) people have no real sympathizers in the community

62. Which of the following parallels between the plow and bereavement counseling is not claimed by the author?

(A) both are innovative technologies

(B) both result in migration of the communities into which the innovations are introduced

(C) both lead to deserts in the space of only one generation

(D) both are tools introduced by outsiders entering existing communities

(E) both appear to be great innovations, but eventually cause breakdown of communities

Passage Set 2: Answers with Explanations

PASSAGE 1

1. (C) The second paragraph shows Spallanzani as responding to and disagreeing with Needham; therefore he is refuting him. Because Spallanzani's results were the opposite of Needham's, neither (A) nor (B) can be right. Answer (D) uses information nowhere mentioned in the passage. Answer (E) attempts to confuse by using words from the passage, but incorrect information about what the passage actually states.

2. (B) The signal phrase "I believe" indicates that personal opinion is being introduced, which has been absent earlier in the passage. The first two paragraphs do not contain an argument, so (A) is incorrect; (C) and (D) are both inaccurate paraphrases; there is no evidence to support (E).

3. (B) The passage explains Pasteur worked logically. He found by experiment that a broth ferments when air admitted in it after boiling. And hence, mentioned that air contained a factor necessary for spontaneous generation of life, or that viable germs were borne in by air and seeded in sterile nutrient broth.

4. (E) The passage reveals that Pasteur, during his experiments, found that after boiling, broth would ferment only when air was admitted into it, and concluded that air contained necessary factors for generations of life or viable germs.

5. (B) The passage conveys that to destroy the doubts of most skeptics, he used water from those deep, clear wells whose waters had been rendered germ free by slow filtration through sandy soil.

6. (C) The passage reveals that man doesn't know how to produce life from germs that float in the air. A germ is from life for life, and a germ is life. Hence the doctrine of spontaneous generation will never recover from the mortal blow of experiment.

7. (B) The passage states that the parade of men who claimed to have "proved" or who resolutely believed in spontaneous generation in the face of proof to the contrary were unreasonable, and their work was shot through with experimental errors.

8. (A) See the last paragraph, which includes the signaling phrase "It seems to me." This rules out (D). Answers (B) and (C) both use ideas not present anywhere in the passage in a way that does not reflect the opinion expressed in paragraph 5.

9. (B) The passage tells that Pasteur's conclusions caused conflict because they seemed simultaneously to support Biblical account of creation while denying a variety of other philosophical systems. The public was caught up in the crossfire of a vigorous series of public lectures and demonstrations by leading exponents of both views, including novelists and their friends.

10. (D) The passage reveals that it is not an exaggeration to say that the emergence of cell theory represents biology's most significant and fruitful advance.

PASSAGE 2

11. (B) The passage stipulates 40% of American population is engaged in the word trade.

12. (B) The passage implies that the wrecking (or bulldozer) technique reveals our language as full of tricky words, some with nineteen different meanings, other which sound alike but differ in sense. For their puns to ring true, gag writers have to know their way around in the language.

13. (A) According to the passage, we have two district levels of languages: familiar and ordinary words, which everybody knows; and elaborate words that we need to know if we are to feel at home in listening and reading today.

14. (B) The passage makes us understand that gag writers often use a long and unusual word as a hinge of joke.

15. (C) The passage makes us understand that gag writers often use a long and unusual word as a hinge of joke or as a peg for situation comedy.

16. (C) The sentence quoted in the question appears at the end of paragraph 5. Notice the sentence before it, which indicates that gag writers must know the language well. This should help to interpret the following sentence. The meaning of "simulate" (to pretend to have a quality) is also crucial here.

17. (B) The gag writers have influenced radio writers, as words like lepidopterist and entomologist occur in famous radio plays.

PASSAGE 3

18. (A) It is evident from the passage that crises in western civilization exist because there has been something wrong with its education. The author believes that no civilization has ever devoted more energy and resources to organized education.

19. (C) The author describes that Lord Snow split the intellectual life of western society between scientists and literary intellectuals because the aim of his education policy was: (a) to get as many alpha-plus scientists as the country can throw up; and (b) to train "a much larger stratum of alpha professionals."

20. (B) The passage uses analysis to support an individual opinion. The point of the passage is clear throughout, so it cannot be called ambiguous (eliminating the final two answers); it does express an opinion, eliminating the first answer, but it does not do so using particularly emotional language, eliminating option (C).

21. (B) According to the author, the existence of more or less fixed ideas in other people's minds - ideas with which they think without being aware of doing so - are called "prejudices."

22. (A) The passage says that if politicians, administrators, and entire communities can at least be educated enough to "make sense" of what the real people, scientists and engineers, are talking about then the gulf of mutual incomprehension between "Two Cultures" will be bridged.

23. (C) Paragraph 3 "......there must be something more to education than Lord Snow suggests."

24. (A) The passage says that the essence of education is the transmission of values. This means that values are more than mere formulae or dogmatic assertion. Instead, we think and feel with them and they are the very instruments through which we interpret and experience the world.

25. (D) He does not express belief in any of the given options.

26. (B) The 4ᵗʰ paragraph notes that the essence of education is the transmission of values. Overall, the author's tone regarding values is positive.

27. (C) The author contends, in the last paragraph, that thinking is generally the application of pre-existing ideas to a given situation or set of facts. Moreover, everywhere else we evaluate the situation in the light of our value ideas.

PASSAGE 4

28. (D) The passage clarifies that the American army was designed to fight on the plains of Europe and thus lost the war because it was not used to fighting in the jungle, while the Vietnamese were on their own land and utilized a different method of warfare.

29. (B) The passage reveals all of the Asian ways of war except this option.

30. (A) The passage clearly states that ever since Sun-tzu, the Chinese have been seen as masters of subtlety who take measured actions to manipulate an adversary without his knowledge.

31. (D) The second to last paragraph illustrates the difference in the two views.

32. (A) The passage clarifies that to the American strategic mind, the Viet Cong guerilla did not fight fairly. They should have come out in open and fought like men, instead of hiding in the jungle and sneaking around like a cat in the night.

33. (C) The passage states that Chinese intervention in Korea and the Tet offensive in Vietnam came out of tradition of surprise and stealth.

PASSAGE 5

34. (A) The passage clearly reveals that in the name of modernization in the west and of development in the third world, the happiness of individuals was to be guaranteed.

35. (E) The passage states that, on the positive side, efforts by certain population groups to assert their identity can be regarded as a "Liberation Movement," challenging oppression and injustice and, on the negative side, militant action for recognition makes such groups more entrenched in their attitudes and makes their cultural compartments more watertight.

36. (D) The passage addresses a serious problem and attempts to suggest solutions, so "earnest" is a good descriptor. Although the passage indicates that the problem is serious, it does not suggest that there's no solution, eliminating answer (A), and although it is generally positive, it does not ignore difficulties, eliminating answer (B). Some emotion is involved, but this does not overly influence the passage, eliminating option (C), and its generally optimistic tone also eliminates (E).

37. (B) The passage reveals that in the name of national unity, equality of all its citizens, and non-partisan secularism, the state can use its powerful resources to reject the demand of the communities; it may even go so far as genocide to ensure order prevails.

38. (C) Options (A), (B), (D) & (E) can be inferred from the passage as the state has failed to guarantee security or social justice and has been unable to prevent international wars. Moreover, the state can use its powerful sources to reject the demand of communities.

PASSAGE 6

39. (C) This can be understood from the first line.

40. (B) See the end of the first paragraph where the author explains that he cannot reveal and produce at the same time.

41. (D) The passage clarifies that there is a difference between perception and creation. In perception, the object is essential and the subject is inessential, whereas in creation, the subject is essential and the object is inessential.

42. (A) The passage reveals that reading is necessary and it lasts as long as the act can last. Beyond that there are only black marks on paper, but the writer can't read what he has written.

43. (B) The first paragraph states "A chief motive of artistic creation is the need to feel we are essential in relationship to the world". And writing is an artistic creation, as mentioned in the last paragraph.

PASSAGE 7

44. (E) The passage expresses that abstract artists were perceived as being incapable of technical drafting skills so they resorted to an art form that was less time consuming. Also, those critical of abstract art believe that art should be real, logical and rational.

45. C) The passage explains that people feel more comfortable with something that they can relate to and understand immediately, without too much thought.

46. (B) It can be understood from the paragraph that if Guernica had used representational imagery it would not have evoked the same emotional response.

47. (C) The passage explains that Mondrian was trying to present a system of simplicity, logic, and rational order. As a result his pieces ended up looking like a scrabble board.

48. (A) The second last paragraph says that both classes of painters have their ways of depicting "reality." To a representational artist, reality is what he sees with his eyes. To an abstract artist, reality is what he feels about what his eyes see.

PASSAGE 8

49. (B) From the second paragraph.

50. (B) From the second paragraph.

51. (A) It is clear from the paragraph that technological methods represent an effort to keep current policies consistent with stated goals, and it is analogous to the effort in GATT to keep contracting party trade practices consistent with stated rules.

52. (D) It should be simple to eliminate options (A), (C), and (E), as they all indicate emotional stances not present in the passage. Choosing between (B) and the best answer, (D), might be more difficult. Most passages can be said to be descriptive in some way, however, analytic is a more precise term. If an issue is being analyzed, it would be a better answer. In the case of this passage, we note that a question is introduced in the first paragraph (Why was the WTO created when it was?) and then a series of factors that help answer the question are presented; this is the classic organization for analysis.

53. (C) It is understood that countries at the Uruguay round placed greater priority on export gains than on import loses, and they came to associate the WTO and a rules-based system with those gains.

54. (D) See the fifth sentence of the third paragraph. The trick to answering this question is to resist choosing answers that appear earlier in the passage. Notice that, as in many cases, the questions follow the order of the passage.

PASSAGE 9

55. (C) While talking about bereavement counseling, the author is predicting the future, hence A is not true.

56. (B) The paragraph gives the traditional method of bereavement handling in which farmers and townspeople mourned at the death of mother, brother, and son, and the bereaved is joined by neighbors and kin. They meet grief together in lamentation, prayer, and song. They also surround themselves in community.

57. (C) The author says that tools of bereavement counseling will create a desert where community once flourished. The bereavement counselor will see the impossibility of restoring hope in clients once they are alone with nothing but a service for consolation. With the failure of bereavement counseling, the counselor will find desert in herself.

58. (D) According to the passage, a bereavement counselor is a person who meets the needs of those experiencing the death of loved ones and one who can process the grief of the people.

59. (A) According to the passage, when they reached Indiana Europeans were puzzled by the environment. Some also called it "Great Desert." It seemed untillable. The earth was wet and it was covered with centuries of tangled and matted grass.

60. (D) The passage clearly says that it took Europeans just one generation to make their homeland into a desert. The Sauk Indians banished themselves to another desert called a reservation. The counselor's new tool will cut through the social fabric throwing aside kinship, care, neighborly obligations, and community ways of coming together and going on. The tools will create a desert where a community once flourished.

61. (A) From the last paragraph.

62. (B) "Migration of communities" with reference to bereavement counseling is not mentioned anywhere in the passage, whereas the other three parallels are mentioned at different points in the passage.

Resources for further Online Practice

You can further enhance your reading skills by regularly going through the following websites:

- CNN
- Economist
- National Geographic
- Fast Company
- NY Times
- Wall Street Journal
- Harvard Business Review
- CNN Money
- Fortune
- Business Week
- The McKinsey Quarterly

These websites publish interesting articles that will push your mind and understanding of varied topics.

Made in United States
North Haven, CT
18 July 2023

39203225R00076